# AROUND THE COAST WITH BUFFALO BILL

## The Wild West in Yorkshire & Lincolnshire

by

James Noble

Hutton Press
1999

Published by
Hutton Press Ltd.
130 Canada Drive, Cherry Burton,
Beverley HU17 7SB


Copyright © 1999

*Printed by Burstwick Print & Publicity Services*
*13a Anlaby Road Hull, HU1 2PJ*


**ISBN   1 902709 03 9**

*BUFFALO BILL - 1892 by kind permission of The Royal Archives*
*and Her Majesty The Queen.*

# AROUND THE COAST WITH BUFFALO BILL
## by James Noble

## CONTENTS

## AROUND THE COAST WITH BUFFALO BILL

With grateful thanks extended to:-

The Buffalo Bill Historical Center, Cody, Wyoming
Mr. David Robinson, of York
Mr. Ian Dewhirst, Mr. A. D. Renshaw, Mr. Chris Leigh (Steam Magazine)
Mr. Arthur Credland, Town Docks Museum, Hull
The Yorkshire and Lincolnshire Libraries and Museums
The Central Library, Manchester
Circus World Museum, Baraboo, Wisconsin
Mr. P. T. Weyell (West Brompton Cemetery)
Mr. & Mrs. D. A. Barber

And many other individuals, too numerous to name, without whose help this book would never have been written.

**And dedicated to the memory of. . .**

The Honourable Colonel W.F. Cody
Mr. Nate Salsbury
Major J. M. Burke: Miss Annie Oakley
Mr. Johnny Baker (The Cowboy Kid): Buck Taylor (King of the Cowboys)
Miss Lillian Smith (The California Girl)
Sitting Bull, Long Wolf, Paul Eagle Star,
John Thomas Percival Noble.

and

The Indians, Cowboys, Mexicans, Scouts,
All the Frontier Ladies
All the sharpshooters
All the Daring Wild Western Riders
The Buffaloes, Elks, Mules, Deer, Burros
And Bucking Horses.

of

BUFFALO BILL'S WILD WEST

HON. W. F. CODY.
(BUFFALO BILL)

# Portrait of a Plainsman
## William Frederick Cody, 'Buffalo Bill'

Over the last hundred years, much has been written about William Frederick Cody, some to his credit and some not. It is probably true to say that many of his documented adventures have been embroidered, not least by himself, but it is also true to say that most of these have their basis in fact. It must be remembered that in the days of the old west a major way of passing the time, in the absence of other entertainment, was the telling of tall tales, and a penchant for this skill at the time could be considered an advantage to a person's popularity.

Whatever else, the researches for this book have shown Cody to be a real gentleman who never let a friend down, and was generous to his own downfall. In the context of the Wild West Show the records show his consideration for both man, beast and pesky reporters.

Cody was born on February 26th 1846, at Leclaire, Scott County, Iowa. He was the second of eight children, born into the hardships and violence of early America. In 1854 his father, an abolitionist, was killed by pro-slavers, forcing the young Will to find a job and help to support the family. He found work in Fort Leavenworth with the freighting company 'Russell, Majors and Waddell as a messenger, but eventually made his way through several jobs, including being a rider for the pony express. Undoubtedly, his early life on the plains was full of adventure and incident and much of this has been documented elsewhere, but it was this very way of life which set the scene for great things to come.

During the Civil War, Cody's enlistment was delayed due to a promise made to his mother. When she died on November 22nd 1863, he joined Company F, the Seventh Kansas Cavalry Regiment under the command of Colonel C. R. Dennison. It was February 19th, 1864, and Cody was seventeen. Because of his background he probably spent most of his military life scouting and reconnoitring, remaining a private until discharged in September 1865.

Prior to the end of Cody's military career he met Louisa Frederici and became close friends with both her and her father, John. Cody's early relationship with Louisa was somewhat strange in that they found it an advantage to be seen as being engaged, although no formal proposals seem to have been made. The arrangement was obviously taken more seriously by Louisa, for a short time later, after Cody had left to find work as a stagecoach driver for the Overland Line, she wrote asking his intentions regarding their marriage and suggested he had not been totally honest. Whatever Cody's original intentions had been, he decided to do the 'gentlemanly' thing, the marriage taking place on March 6th 1866.

Settling at first in Salt Creek Valley, Cody made a vain attempt at hotel - keeping, but the life quickly palled for him and after moving Louisa into the home of her sister, set out west for adventure and to seek his fortune. He met William Rose at Ellsworth, and the two decided to speculate on the site of a new town which would take advantage of the expansion of the railroads, but the tracks wound towards Hays City and the venture was doomed.

We can only speculate from the many stories how Cody really obtained the name of 'Buffalo Bill'. He hunted these magnificent animals and sold the meat himself in Hays City, but was also employed by contractors to the railroads to provide meat for the workers. In this capacity, it has been said that Cody would drive a herd of buffalo toward the tracks before shooting them, avoiding the need for a wagon to go out to recover the carcasses. Twelve buffalo per day were required and over an eighteen-month period, according to Cody himself, he killed 4280 animals. His pay was $500 per month but the tally was probably an exaggeration.

Cody also took part in contests with other hunters, probably the most famous of which being the one with William Comstcock,

*Buffalo Bill (Circa 1888).*

also known as 'Medicine Bill' in which the two vied for the title of 'Champion Buffalo Killer'. Side bets were apparently numerous over the one-day hunt culminating with Cody taking sixty-nine animals to Comstock's forty-six. Some doubts exist as to whether the match actually took place, Medicine Bill being wanted at the time for the killing of an unarmed man at Fort Wallace.

There were several other men on the frontier that had coined the name of 'Buffalo Bill' but whatever the origin it was certainly in Cody that the title found its true nemesis. By 1868, Cody was working for the army as a scout, first for the 10th and then the 5th Cavalry Regiment. His adventures were many and he was soon highly regarded by many well-known military officers of the day. During this period Cody acted as guide and scout for the Grand Duke Alexis in a frontier hunting trip. Also on hand was another name that would soon be famous, George Armstrong Custer.

Cody had become acquainted in 1869 with Ned Buntline (Edward Judson), the familiar writer of many 'frontier fantasies', some soon to be based around the character of Buffalo Bill. Seeing the possibilities in the eastern theatres, Buntline persuaded Cody to take to the stage in his play, 'Scouts of the Prairie'. Opening on 17th December 1872, the show rightly received a bad press for the performances of the cast, but never-the-less, due to the fact that the 'real' Buffalo Bill and Co. were participating, each presentation played to a packed house. The season closed in June 1873 with Cody somewhat disappointed with his pay as an actor and returning to the west was reunited with his family.

By September, Buffalo Bill was back on the stage in 'Scouts of the Prairie', this time with Wild Bill Hickok in a supporting role. Hickok, not liking his acting career to any great extent, disgraced himself with rough behaviour on stage and was asked by Cody and fellow thespian 'Texas Jack Omahundro' to leave. The parting was amicable and the show continued until 1876, the year that Cody's son, Kit Carson Cody died of scarlet fever.

Disheartened with his stage career, Cody acceded to requests to join General Crook as a scout. Invasion by gold prospectors in the Black Hills, which were sacred to the Sioux, was contrary to the treaty of 1868. Custer had led an expedition through the area in 1874 and reporting the finding of gold, thereby initiated the influx of thousands of gold hungry whites and the setting up of unlawful settlements. The Sioux not un-naturally regarded the treaty as thereby null and void and began to leave the confinements of the reservation, and it was to resolve this situation that Crook and his command was charged. Cody joined the 5th Cavalry shortly before the demise of Custer at Little Big Horn, (known to the Sioux as the 'Greasy Grass'), and en route to Fort Laramie with the regiment he was involved in a skirmish with the Cheyenne, culminating in the famous duel with Yellow Hand, an event which would be re-enacted in the Wild West (show) in later years.

While appearing on eastern stages, Cody had met Nate Salsbury, actor businessman and to some extent, entrepreneur. Salsbury saw the possibilities in expanding the stage presentations, having had thoughts of an equestrian exhibition while travelling in Australia. Back in Nebraska, Cody had staged the 'Old Glory Blowout' in 1882, a Fourth of July celebration including Indians, buffalo and cowboys, all of the elements of the future Wild West, and this is discussed in further detail in the next section.

Cody set up the fledgling Wild West in partnership with 'Doc' Carver, opening early in 1883 at Omaha, Nebraska. Salsbury was invited to join them but he disliked Carver intensely and demurred, being bitterly disappointed but keeping an eye on the progress of the show. Carver and Cody disagreed constantly and before long decided to part company, the ownership of the components of the show decided by the flipping of a coin. Luckily for Cody, he won the old Deadwood stagecoach.

Buffalo Bill then approached Salsbury once more and together with Adam Bogardus, formed a management team to run the 'Wild West'. Bogardus quickly dropped out of the scene, leaving the other two, and after a somewhat rocky beginning, they settled into a long partnership which lasted until the death of Salsbury in 1902.

The relationship between Cody and his wife broke down in February 1905 with Louisa beginning divorce proceedings against him. Although there was certainly some affection between them, the marriage had never been a totally happy affair and all the wrongs that Louisa felt had been done to her over the years were now thrown at Buffalo Bill. Indeed, there must have been some justification in her feelings, sometimes playing second fiddle to Cody's business interests and the situation not improved by his dalliances with 'ladies of the stage'.

Cody took the stand on March 6th, his thirty - ninth wedding anniversary, and made a poor representation to the court. It has also been said that in court Louisa cited Queen Victoria as one of many who vied for Cody's affections, but in fact the true version is that she simply resented the attention shown Buffalo Bill by many lady admirers, including the Queen. After somewhat odd allegations and evidence, Judge Scott ruled in favour of Louisa, with Cody having to pay all costs, and the situation remained thus until July 1910 when the family managed to reunite them.

The rest, as the saying goes, is now history, and in the following pages more of the story is revealed. Whatever we may think of Cody it is undoubtedly his personality that was stamped upon the Wild West (show) and certainly the modern concept of recent American history to some extent is shaped by the way that he wished it to be seen. With the advent of more detailed research we now know that the truth is less picturesque and clean cut, but we must also bear in mind that Cody sought to bring many good values to the show's audiences, even if only to enhance his own image. Triumph of good over evil, courage, honesty and the American way may seem corny to us today but to those entering the turnstiles ninety or more years ago, Buffalo Bill was the image which captured just those values. If we cannot admire the man or what he was, then perhaps we can admire the achievements of the great show that he came to represent. . .

**. . .The Wild West**

*Buffalo Bill*

*Buffalo Bill*

# WELCOME TO THE WILD WEST

*Natural and Realistic Scenes on the Far Frontier of the United States with Indians, Scouts, Cowboys, Vaqueros, Riflemen, Western Girls. . .*
*Everything Natural! No Guilding! No Humbug!*

Although he is a major character in what follows this is not just a story of Buffalo Bill, and it is not the intention of this book to sway the reader toward one aspect of his character or another. The following pages will, however, give detailed insight into an enterprise in which he was probably the greatest influence over its thirty year existence. More specifically it is an explanation of the mechanics, organisation, personnel and politics of the show with emphasis on its life and experiences in Yorkshire and Lincolnshire. Where appropriate information outside this area is given for the interest of the reader and also to give fuller account of the Wild West and outside influences upon it.

Buffalo Bill's Wild West was not as some think a circus, for the simple reason that those taking part were not actors as such, but the actual participants in real events. Also, the show had a definite theme and was not just a series of skilful but unlinked performances. The cowboys and Indians, for example, were just that and indeed some of the latter who performed in such re-enactments as 'Custer's Last Stand', were actually there at the Little Big Horn on that day. The Wild West became one of the most successful (artistically if not financially) and unique of the travelling shows both in the United States and in Europe, making Buffalo Bill the traditional western icon that we accept even today. It must also be remembered that the show was presented prior to the advent of television and feature films and so the impact on audiences of the period must have been quite substantial.

Even as the Wild West thrilled the public in its heyday, the true West was disappearing fast. Gone were the buffalo which once roamed the prairies in their tens of millions, gone the free-wheeling plains tribes with their colourful traditions and gone many of the frontier characters such as Cody. Much that was, and still is written, about the people of the early American frontier is either pure nonsense, prefabrication or exaggeration, first conjured up by the dime novels and later enlarged even more by the magic of television and Hollywood. Many of the traditional western characters that we know so well owe their fame (or notoriety) to a few minor incidents which have been enlarged and elaborated to become a lifetime of adventure. While it is true that Buffalo Bill's life has been exaggerated, and not least by himself, it is also true that there is an element of truth in all of the stories. He rode for the Pony Express, served as a scout for the Army, hunted buffalo for the Railroads, took part in significant engagements in the Indian Wars and not least became one of the most legendary showmen in recent history.

The real star, however is the 'Wild West'. The show experienced successes and failures, good times and bad and endured for thirty years, but Buffalo Bill's exhibition was not the first to explore the genre. In 1843 Barnum, later better known for his circus connections, bought a small group of buffalo and organised a 'Buffalo Hunt' at Hoboken, New Jersey. Also on the bill were Indian dances and a western menagerie. Over twenty thousand people attended, showing the potential for the larger western shows to come, and Barnum himself planned an even greater exhibition for 1860 which was not realised.

On 28th, and 30th August 1872, 'Wild Bill' Hickok was persuaded to take part, as Master of Ceremonies, in a 'Grand Buffalo Hunt' staged on the Canadian side of the Niagara Falls. The buffalo were reported to have been captured at the foot of the Rocky Mountains and the event was to take part on a specially constructed park. As the Government refused to allow a troupe of Pawnee to leave their reservation to participate in the show, the organisers obtained warriors of the Sac and Fox tribes. Also taking part were Mexicans who showed their skills with the lariat by roping Texas steers.

There were several other western shows over the years, and some circuses and variety theatres in England included tableaux depicting the 'Wild Frontier' of America. When the Wild West made its first performance in Hull in May 1888, Hengler's Cirque, situated on the city's Anlaby Road, was offering as top billing, 'The Far-West' with performances at 2.30p.m. and 7.30 p.m. By today's standards, Hengler's seems a strange mixture of vaudeville and circus. Having auditoriums in many large cities, it often presented items of topical interest such as 'Stanley's discovery of Livingstone', 'The Fall of Khartoum' or indeed the 'Wild West', and included animals such as horses and monkeys. Sometimes the billposters advertised exhibitions by famous pugilists, boxer of the period. The week after Buffalo Bill left Hull in 1888, Mitchell and Kilrain, an Englishman and an American, stood toe to toe in the city's 'Carr Laneries'. Hengler's stood next to the Palace theatre and was eventually destroyed by fire.

Sanger's Circus, owned by George Sanger also capitalised on Cody's fame on this side of the Atlantic by including 'Scenes from Buffalo Bill' in his show. This western pageant boasted several real buffaloes, Indians and a stagecoach, although the authenticity of the latter two items is open to question. When Cody came to England and saw the blatant advertising using his name and his show he encouraged his agents to cover the posters with his own. Sanger persisted and was served an injunction by Buffalo Bill, the two coming eye to eye in London's High Court in 1887. Before Mr. Justice Chitty, Sanger agreed not to use the Wild West advertising in a way that would infer that Cody's show was part of his own, but would later not be totally true to his promise. Some legal wranglings followed and eventually Sanger was surprisingly allowed to use the terms 'Buffalo Bill' and 'Wild West' providing he made it clear that there was no connection with Cody and his enterprise. Cody no doubt saw the advantages in someone else giving him publicity. In his published programmes Sanger still insisted in using very similar descriptions and illustrations to those by Cody. Buffalo Bill was still unhappy with the outcome but at least Sanger was ordered to pay the costs. One amusing follow on to the story is that during the Court hearing, Buffalo Bill was continually being referred to as the 'Honourable' Colonel Cody, a title to which he was certainly due, being elected to the State Legislature of Nebraska. Sanger was considerably irritated by the term and apparently remarked that 'if Cody was the HONOURABLE Colonel Cody, then he was LORD George Sanger', and so Lord George Sanger he became from then on.

In later years, the famous Beverley artist Fred Elwell and his wife travelled with Sanger's circus and in a painting to be seen hanging in the Beverley Art Gallery, Yorkshire, Elwell admirably depicts the line of horses in the stable tent. This gives same idea of the atmosphere of the period and how Buffalo Bill's own horse accommodation would have looked, although considerably larger.

Cody's stage performances in the East Coast of America had enhanced his fame. Spending the winters in the theatre, he still chose to return to the west in the summer, sometimes wearing the same costumes that he had worn for performances in New York. With 'Texas Jack' Omahundo, in what was called 'The Buffalo Bill Combination', he had persuaded 'Wild Bill' Hickok to join them in September 1873 in a play called 'Scouts of the Plains' by Fred Maeder. Hickok never liked the actor's life and disgraced himself by firing blanks close to the legs of supporting actors, and eventually was asked by Cody to leave the show. The split was amicable with Cody and the rest of the cast making a parting gift to Hickok of money and a pair of Remington pistols.

On 4th July 1882, Cody organised a rudimentary Wild Western show to celebrate Independence Day at North Platte, Nebraska, which he called the 'Old Glory Blow-Out'. Using local cowboys and real Indians, he persuaded the town worthies to put up prizes for several of the events, with Cody chasing a small herd of buffalo around the settlement's race track for atmosphere. The event was a great success and some believe this to be the origin of the present day rodeo. Whether this is true or not, it must surely have put the seeds of something bigger into Cody's mind.

In 1883, together with 'Doc' W. F. Carver, Cody was organising a Wild West proper with both putting in a considerable sum of money of which Carver's contribution was $27,000. Born in 1846, the same year as Cody, Carver had been a dentist and later became an exhibition sharpshooter. Cody had met Nate Salsbury some years earlier and discussed the possibilities of such a show but neither at the time had the financial muscle necessary to put their ideas into action. Salsbury was an actor/producer of some ability who at times toured with his own company and also saw the possibilities for a western show, although his idea was far more of an equestrian exhibition.

With Carver's agreement Cody, who could see the advantage of Salsbury's business acumen, contacted the latter and offered him a share in the Wild West. Salsbury disliked Carver intensely and declined. To all accounts, Carver was prone to be untruthful, at one time claiming the honour of inventing the title 'Wild West', and also saying that he had wanted to call the show 'The Golden West'. In order to smooth out the growing uneasiness between them, they agreed to call it 'Cody and Carver's Wild West' although it was sometimes billed as 'Hon. W. F. Cody and Dr. W. F. Carver's Rocky Mountain and Prairie Exhibition'.

To augment the company of Indians, cowboys and other western characters, Cody managed to obtain the original Deadwood Stagecoach which had come upon sad times after an Indian attack and been left derelict. It was repaired and reconditioned and became the stuff of legend, twice daily, rain or shine.

Cody's idea was for a show which would amplify his own background and in particular himself as part of it, and who can blame him. At a time when there were no welfare systems it was up to the individual to take the responsibility for his own destiny. Some did so by turning to crime and perhaps worse, but Buffalo Bill's way was by giving his patrons good times and memories at a small cost. A more realistic criticism would be that the Wild West did not really show the west as it historically was, and certainly the publicity for the show claimed it to do just that. However, the image of the frontier had already been established, however inaccurate, by the dime novels. Of course, Cody had also been a part of these publications and this has added further-weight to the arguments put forward by his critics over the years. On the other hand, the Wild West had many positive points, which must be born in mind. It projected the theory of good

against evil toward the many children who would visit the show, not just by the vehicle of cowboy versus Indian but also showing that there were bad whites to be overcome in scenes such as 'The Great Train Hold Up' and 'Dealing with a Horse Thief'.

Especially in later years, Indians in the show were shown in two distinct themes. Firstly they were portrayed as the traditional 'enemy' to be overcome, although in such events such as 'Custer's Last Stand' they were allowed to be shown as the victors. Of course this was after a particularly heroic defence on the part of the Seventh Cavalry. Indians were also shown as a people with their own culture and traditions in various sections of the show, a fact which is often forgotten. In the early days of the Wild West this was mainly by giving individuals the chance to show their prowess in horsemanship, but later whole sections of the performance were given over to displaying various aspects of the more peaceful side of the plains Indians. Also, the public were encouraged to visit the Indian encampment after the show, seeing them closely at first hand, and while this might at first seem to turn them into a side-show, it must be remembered that there are some references to the Indians looking upon their visitors in the same way and using the occasion to sell Postcards and artefacts.

The Wild West opened in Omaha, Nebraska on 17th May 1883 (some references make it the 19th), and played before eight thousand people. Already part of the show were the beginnings of the Grand Revue, the attack on the Deadwood Coach, the inclusion of the buffalo and the engagements between whites and Indians. The giant Buck Taylor joined the show, and would carve his own niche in western lore in the years to come. Also Gordon Lillie, who would assume the title of 'Pawnee Bill' and have his own spectacle, which in the future would join forces with the Wild West. Lillie joined the show as an interpreter and stayed for one season. Others taking part included Fred Matthews who drove the Deadwood Stagecoach; Johnny Baker, the youngster who idolised Cody and who would himself become a sharpshooter and vital link in the running of the Wild West; Captain A. H. Bogardus and his four sons, also sharpshooters, and Major Frank North, one of the true, if little known heroes of the frontier.

The sequence for the opening of the show took on a format which would, generally speaking, remain for the next thirty years.

1) Opening Revue.
2) Races on bareback range ponies.
3) The Pony Express demonstration.
4) Indian attack on the Deadwood Stagecoach.
5) Race between Indians on foot and horseback.
6) Sharpshooting by Captain Bogardus.
7) Sharpshooting by Cody and Carver.
8) Races between Cowboys on range ponies.
9) Cowboy Fun / Bronc riding etc.
10) Texas steer riding.
11) Buffalo roping and riding.
12) Grand Buffalo Hunt and final Indian Battle.

During the first tour of 1883 in the United States, the show barely managed to meet expenses. Cody and Carver could agree on hardly any facet of the partnership and eventually, when the Wild West returned to Omaha, they decided to split. Flipping a coin to decide the ownership of the assets of the show, Cody , by good fortune, became the owner of the Deadwood stagecoach. Nate Salsbury, who had followed the fortunes of the Wild West closely, now came back into the picture. After a contract was drawn up by a young German lawyer named John Peter Altgeld, Salsbury became Cody's partner, vice president and general manager. Also joining the show at this time was John M. Burke (Arizona John), who filled the role of business manager, and brilliant press agent. Burke admired Cody to the point of hero worship, as can be seen in his writings in subsequent programme publications, words which seem to go beyond what was really necessary, even for publicity purposes.

At first, there was some discord between Cody and Salsbury, but the two quickly settled into a successful partnership which would last until Salsbury's death in 1902. Salsbury brought organisation to the Wild West in the form of rules and regulations for the cast (including Cody), efficient accounting and a thorough knowledge of touring with a show. Captain Bogardus was also invited to become a partner, and did so but remained for only one season. He seems to have added little to the enterprise, either artistically or in a managerial capacity.

In the meantime, a disgruntled and embittered Carver continued to harass Cody by way of verbal attacks, making the accusation that Buffalo Bill was continually drunk and did little to further the interests of the show. While there is no doubt that both men were inclined to take a drink or two, the 'spirit' of Carver's remarks were for the most part unfounded, and it is perhaps a sign that most of the staff and performers elected to remain with Cody.

In 1884, the Wild West played St. Louis, Chicago and New York, and that year, while being transported by riverboat down the Mississippi, the vessel collided with another boat, near a place called Rodney and sank. There are several versions of the story, but one detail common to each was the fact that most of the show was lost. The Deadwood Stagecoach was saved but much of the props and some of the stock was lost beneath thirty feet of water. Amazingly, Cody managed to obtain replacements and opened at the next venue on time. 1884 ended with the show owing $60,000. Cody told Salsbury, who was still touring away with his own show at the time, that he would give it one more year.

*Typical illustrations from the programme sold on the showground.*

More changes were now made to the show with the inclusion of Annie Oakley and her husband and manager, Frank Butler. Also at that time came Frank Richmond, as narrator, whose superb voice would soon impress even Queen Victoria.

By 1885, the Wild West was solvent again and a huge success, playing over forty venues in the US and Canada. That same year, on June 6th, Sitting Bull was persuaded by Major Burke to tour with the show, by assuring him that he would see Annie Oakley every day. Sitting Bull had met Annie and had been impressed by her shooting abilities, calling her 'Little Sure Shot'. The famous Indian Chief, a Hunkpapa Sioux, stayed with the show for four months at a wage of $50 per week and a franchise to sell his own autographs and postcards. American audiences, still bearing the memory of Custer's defeat, felt little empathy for him or his part in the show, but in Canada he was cheered heartily an entering the arena. When Sitting Bull left the Wild West, Cody replaced him with Red Shirt, another notable Sioux Chieftain.

A six month period at Erastina on Staten Island followed in 1886, during which time Cody signed up Lillian Smith, 'The California Girl'. Although the show had many sharpshooters, Lillian was said to be the equal of Annie Oakley, and perhaps Buffalo Bill already suspected that Annie had other ambitions. Only fourteen when recruited by Cody, Lillian Smith travelled to England with the show in 1887 and although she lacked Annie Oakley's personality and ability to relate to an audience, was very well received by the English crowds.

The Wild West attracted many celebrities among the rich and famous, actors and politicians. Among them was Mark Twain, author of 'Huckleberry Finn' and 'Tom Sawyer'. Twain greatly admired the show, and it was he who encouraged Cody and Salsbury to take the Wild West to England, where he was certain of its success. During his stage career, Cody had considered coming to England, but other pseudo-westerners had preceded him, and he feared being branded as a charlatan.

*Annie Oakley and Indians posing on man-made scenery at Earle's Court in 1887.*

1887 was to be Queen Victoria's Jubilee, and to celebrate, many fine exhibitions and demonstrations were to be staged in London. One of these was the 'Exhibition of the Arts, Industries, Manufactures, Products and resources of the United States', otherwise known by the easier title of 'The American Exhibition'.

*Reproduced from a programme, the photograph shows the cast at Earle's court. In the area between the two flagpoles (right) are Cody, Annie Oakley, Lillian Smith and to the left, Buck Taylor.*

The directors, knowing of Buffalo Bill from the popular 'Penny Dreadfuls', had little doubt that the Wild West would prove as popular and offered the opportunity for the show to appear in London for six months as part of the American exhibition. The Wild West in return would give over a percentage of its Box

Office receipts. With little argument, Cody and Salsbury agreed, and thus began the first visit of the Wild West to England; to London, to Birmingham, to Manchester, and ultimately for the first time to Yorkshire. The company left America on the steamship 'State of Nebraska', landed at Gravesend, and was transported upon three trains to the Midland Station, close to the exhibition showgrounds.

The American exhibition in general was perhaps a little 'dry' for the general public and did not excite Londoners as much as it might have, but the Wild West certainly did. Crowds thronged to the showgrounds for some time before the opening performances and on April 28th, Mr. Gladstone visited with his wife, and after touring the Indian encampment, lunched with Buffalo Bill and the company in the dining tent. Royalty also patronised the Wild West, including the Queen and the Prince of Wales, bestowing gifts upon Cody and other members of the show, and elevating them to the heights of fashionable London society.

BUFFALO BILL'S WILD WEST made several visits to Yorkshire and Lincolnshire between 1887 and 1904, visiting eventually most major towns and cities. It is not just a story of wild rides and gunfire, ships and trains, Indians and buffalo, but also a parade of interesting local incidents which have almost been lost to time.

But not quite...

BRANDED BY BUFFALO BILL
OR
THE BRIMSTONE BROTHERHOOD

"The revolver was pointed straight at him, and the words came sharp and stern, 'Edmund Allyn, you are my prisoner. I AM Buffalo Bill!'"

*Above: A 'penny dreadful' featuring Buffalo Bill.*
*Left: Indian Teepee (reproduced from the programme).*

# WILD MEN AND WILD HORSES

*A description of the Wild West as it would have appeared to the audiences in Yorkshire and Lincolnshire and how it developed during the visits of 1887/8, 1891 and 1903/4.*

Imagine the scene. You have come far, with anticipation growing as you walk the final few yards towards the appointed time and place. You have read the dime novels and heard the stories and now here you are, about to see for yourself, the Wild West as it really was. The Indians, the cowboys, the buffalo, and the actual Deadwood Stagecoach.

The crowds increase, until when almost at the showground, it becomes a heaving mass of people desperate not to miss one second of the coming entertainment. Some have tickets, others do not, hoping to buy one at the gate or sneak a free glimpse from some high vantage point.

Beyond the canvas walling which surrounds the arena, the Cowboy Band plays stirring marches to pacify the fifteen thousand waiting for the afternoon show to begin.

At last you are in your seat beneath the dark red awnings which shade you from the warm afternoon sun and flags of all nations flutter above the canopies. Before you, the long rectangular arena stretches left and right, with spectators along three sides. The remaining short side is draped with a beautifully painted backdrop by the famous American artist, Frederick Dangerfield, depicting a distant western scene with mountains, rivers and pine trees. As the time to begin draws near, the noise of the crowd increases.

Then, with typical punctuality, the Cowboy Band begins to play a rousing version of the 'Star Spangled Banner', and suddenly, the backdrop folds back as into the arena, screaming and yelling from the backs of their fast little ponies, come a band of painted Cheyenne, whirling their feathered lances. They are followed by another group, Sioux, wearing feathered warbonnets, then a squadron of cowboys and a group of Mexican vaqueros in their broad, felt sombreros. More Indians and cowboys follow, then Arabs, Cossacks, Samurai, English Lancers, United States Cavalry and a detachment of Roosevelt's Rough Riders, until the arena is a seething mass of horsemen, circling three or four times.

The action ceases a little as the riders form regular lines, all but filling the arena. The crowd hushes, as from the far entrance, a big grey horse lazily canters onto the field. On its back is a figure that is well known, even to those who had never actually seen him before, dressed in light buckskins with a wide-brimmed hat. The crowd roars and cheers. William F. Cody, 'Buffalo Bill' himself, urges his horse down toward the far end of the arena past the cheering audience. He halts in front of the lines of horsemen and salutes the crowds with a sweep of his hat. As the cheering finally dies he calls out to his admirers...

"Children, Ladies and Gentlemen, allow me to introduce to you a congress of Rough Riders of the world..."

So began the traditional opening to Buffalo Bill's Wild West as it would have appeared around 1903. Between 1887/8 and the later UK tours of 1891 and 1903/4, the show changed in format from a purely western entertainment to a more universal presentation, with the addition of groups of the world's finest horsemen, but the opening revue, headed by Cody, remained constant and was part of the superb publicity machine that Buffalo Bill and his staff were so good at. The audience was built up from the first moment into a crescendo of excitement that continued non-stop throughout the performance. The only complaint voiced by many who saw the show was that it was over far too quickly. This might have been a valid observation during the early years when the Wild West show was simply that, and lasted an hour and a quarter, but certainly not in subsequent visits when, with new additions, it lengthened to over two hours in duration.

So what was this western whirlwind which captured British, European and North American audiences for thirty years? And what might audiences have seen after paying the modest price of entry into the grounds...?

## Buffalo Bill's Wild West - (Circa 1891)

To give a general overview of the developing show, we must begin in the years when it was well established. After Buffalo Bill's introduction before the grandstand (and usually the most expensive seats), and at a signal from him, the riders in the arena would burst into action, wheeling and circling in a ballet of horseflesh. The audience would be transfixed at the colourful pageant of painted horses, feathers and glinting sabres known as 'The Maze', which was arrayed only a few yards before them. Then, the orator would call through his large brass megaphone...

1—Annie Oakley shooting at clay pigeons.
2—Lilian Smith firing at running deer. 3—Pony express

"Wild West. Are you ready? .... Then Go!"

With the slickness of Mercury, the arena would empty and before the dust settled, the orator would introduce the individual celebrities and groups. Annie Oakley and Lillian Smith, crack rifle shots; Buck Taylor, King of the Cowboys; Johnny Baker, the Cowboy Kid; John Y. Nelson and his Indian family; Captain Fred Matthews, driver of the Deadwood Stage; Scouts, wranglers and vaqueros. Also, to the increased delight of the crowds, individual groups of Indians, each announced with their own Chieftain, giving full name and title. Sioux, Arapahoe, Cheyenne and Brule, all with their fine feathers and warpaint, and riding superb range ponies. Although Cody would later be criticised for his treatment of the Indians in the show, it is only proper to emphasise the fact that by introducing them thus, he changed the general ideas that existed about Native Americans at that time. Instead of continually portraying them as bloodthirsty savages, Cody showed them as a people with their own individual culture and way of life. This was reinforced by

*Left: A page from a souvenir childrens book sold on the show ground depicting the lady sharpshooters and pony express act.*

*Below: This photograph shows cowboys from the 101 Ranch Wild West in 1914. After the sale of Buffalo Bill's show some performers, including Johnny Baker, joined the 101.*

the way that the public were encouraged to visit the Indian encampment on the back lot before and after the show. A good publicity idea, certainly, but one which was beneficial to both parties. That is not to say, however, that the more warlike side of the Indians was not used by Buffalo Bill when it suited him. If a sympathetic view of them was given in some aspects, a different light was cast upon them when the warriors took part in the big battle scenes, where they were nearly always beaten and driven off by cowboys and scouts, 'in the nick of time'.

The first act proper was races between Cheyenne on their wiry little ponies, cowboys on their range horses and Mexicans with their Spanish bloods. During the races there was some good natured rivalry between the riders, cutting each other off at the corners and vying for an inside position. Sadly, history has not passed down the general outcome of the races but it is a fair assumption that the Indian ponies would acquit themselves well.

A burst of applause would then herald the appearance of Annie Oakley, the famous sharpshooter named 'Little Sureshot' by her illustrious admirer, Sitting Bull. It was apparently a fairly short exhibition of marksmanship, but one which never failed to impress the audience. Mainly it comprised of the shattering of glass balls and clay pigeons, accomplished by Annie firing from a plethora of unusual positions. She fired with such rapidity that those who saw her were of the opinion that she aimed and fired at the same instant, which is probably close to the truth. On one occasion she shattered a record 4,772 out of 5000. Annie always appeared early in the show to accustom the crowds to gunfire, much more of which would come later. On occasion, ladies watching had been known to faint at the first shots.

One trick shot was done with the aid of a mirror, or sometimes a Bowie knife, the rifle being discharged over her shoulder, sighting via the reflection. In the arena with Annie, as helpers, and sometimes targets, were her husband and manager, Frank Butler, and their pet poodle, from whose head Annie would shoot an apple. In a further demonstration of her ability, Annie Oakley would split a playing card held sideways by Butler, with a .22 pistol. Then, after tossing four glass balls into the air, she would leap the small table with a green cover, upon which lay her guns, and turning to pick up the rifle, could usually break each one. The act also included shooting coins thrown up by Butler, or sometimes members of the public. The twisted discs were then cold stamped with the word 'Oakley' and given to members of the audience. When complimentary tickets were issued they were punched with a hole, and eventually became known as 'Oakleys'.

*Left: Johnny Baker.*

Annie Oakley used several types of guns but perhaps the one with which she was best known was the Winchester .44 W.C.F. - Model 1873. This was a smoothbore, lever action repeating rifle . Records show Annie's weapon to have been received 'in warehouse' on February 13th, 1888. Its number was 256170B, model number three with a special, colour-hardened finish to the metal parts. On the lower tang was stamped the number 1527XX. It had a plain trigger but with a suede hand protector on the underlever. Annie was only five feet tall and the stock was configured to her size, being a half inch shorter than normal. The barrel, however, was a standard 20" with a full length magazine and non-standard fore and rear sights. The Winchester weighed eight pounds. During her tour of England with the Wild West, Annie and Frank Butler became friendly with Richard Edward Clarke, escaping the rigours of the show occasionally by staying on his estate near Shrewsbury in Shropshire. In 1891, Annie presented Clarke's son, William, with the Winchester, showing her close links with the family. The rifle remained with the Clarkes until its auction at Christies in London on Wednesday, 24th March, 1993. An Oakley penny found £1,380 and the Winchester £84,000. On the stock of the gun is a brass plate bearing the inscription , 'Presented by Annie Oakley to W.R.C. Clarke - 1891'. The Clarke family still retain other souvenirs of Annie's visits, a new England clock, with striking alarm, by E.N. Welch, and a mounted pheasant head which she shot herself. A 'Shooting Times' of 1887 recorded Annie's visits with the Clarkes and noted her being presented with a gold medal by the Schultze Powder Company, her fourth since landing in England.

*Left: Another programme illustration showing Cody shooting glass balls from the back of a galloping horse. The rider throwing the balls is possibly Johnny Baker.*

*Below: One of the glass balls used as targets in the show. A fifty pence piece gives an idea of scale.*

The crowds always loved Annie and in her seventeen years with the Wild West, she only missed performances on four occasions when an insect bite caused an ear infection. It has been said that Buffalo Bill could be a little jealous of her popularity with the public, and there may be some substance to the stories. In 1888, after a quarrel with Cody, Annie left the show before the last performance in England (Hull) that year. She left to pursue a career alone and remained in England after the show left for home, and gave shooting exhibitions all over the country.

Other trick shooters also appeared with the show. Johnny Baker, billed as the Cowboy kid and protege of Cody himself, was also a regular rifle shot. He could break braces of clay pigeons from unusual stances, including standing on his head. As part of the showmanship he would assume this position, then stand again and remove a large rock, rubbing his head to the amusement of the audience. Claude E. Daly changed the style with his superb handling of pistols, and wooed the ladies with his 'prodigious biceps'.

And then came Buffalo Bill with his own exhibition of shooting from the saddle. He would gallop at a pace around the arena, accompanied by another rider (sometimes Baker) who would toss glass balls of approximately four inches in diameter into the air, which would then be shattered by the scout. The balls were made daily on the showground from glass, resin and sulphur. They were filled with various things for effect, such as shredded tissue, coloured powder or small woollen pom-poms. During the course of the show, many of these balls were broken and we can only imagine what minor injuries may have been caused by someone stepping on the debris. Perhaps the inclusion of sulphur and resin helped to change the nature of the composition, but on examination, the balls do seem very glass-like.

Occasionally, Cody and other marksmen would miss their target, but this did not seem to detract from the enjoyment of the audience. Possibly, sometimes a miss was fortunate, extracting greater applause when the shooter succeeded on a second attempt. It was intimated by some that Cody used special trick firearms, machined to assist his aim, but the statement was completely refuted by Johnny Baker, years later. Pawnee Bill, a contemporary of Cody who had his own show which would later merge with the Wild West, certainly did use such weapons. Even had it been the case that Cody had used them, hitting four inch balls from the back of a galloping horse was no mean feat. The programmes announced Cody as a general, all-round shot and certainly the newspaper reports indicate that he was indeed a first class marksman, describing him as...

"Buffalo Bill, the Master Exponent of Horseback Marksmanship in his wonderful exhibition of shooting while riding a galloping horse".

Only the sharpshooters in the show fired shot. Participants in other events such as the historical set-pieces, used blanks.

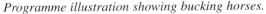

*Programme illustration showing bucking horses.*

The first of these major set-pieces came next and was the re-enactment of the famous duel between Cody and the Sioux war chief, Yellow Hand. The actual incident took place on July 17th, 1876 at Hat Creek (War Bonnet Creek), South Dakota. The Black Hills, sacred to the Sioux, were over-run with prospectors after the discovery of gold, a flagrant violation of the treaty of 1868. The tribes subsequently began to leave the reservations and in May 1876, a full scale military solution to the problem was in preparation. On June 25th, Custer and the 7th Cavalry were wiped out at the Little Big Horn. Cody had joined the 5th Cavalry as a scout under General Carr. The regiment was ordered to move to join General Crook's command at Fort Laramie, and on the way, when hostiles were sighted, the famous incident took place. Yellow Hand is sometimes referred to as Yellow Hair, but his true Sioux name was Hay-o-Wei. As the story goes, the two protagonists rode toward each other at the gallop, opening fire when in range. Buffalo Bill's shot hit the Indian in the leg, killing his horse at the same moment. Then Cody's horse fell, throwing him to the ground, but rising quickly, fired again and killed Yellow Hand. Cody then apparently took the scalp of his opponent and holding the trophy high, called out to the watching soldiers, "The first scalp for Custer!" Several other people present at the incident claimed it for themselves but there is little doubt that Cody was the true slayer of Yellow Hand. In the arena, Cody relived the event with his usual style, adding (inaccurately) hand to hand combat with knife and tomahawk. Possibly to reinforce his claim to the incident, the piece was billed as 'The famous single combat with Yellow Hand in the presence of the Indian and American troops. Generally speaking, in many ways, Cody attained a reputation for authenticity in many of his portrayals of western life and history, but when it came to those parts of the show which affected the way that audiences perceived his own life, he was not adverse to a little exaggeration.

Next on the programme came an illustration of the Pony Express, showing 'the mode of conveying mails on the frontier, in which a rider (Charlie Duprez in 1887 and later Jim Hathaway) would gallop once around the arena, while others working around a mock-up of a line shack would be preparing the next horse. As the mail rider dismounted, he would immediately urge his next mount into a canter, leaping into the saddle as it picked up speed. The rider carried a mochilla, a type of saddle-bag especially designed for carrying mail which could be thrown over the horse's neck. Although given much space in the books of western history, not to mention the hype of Hollywood, the Pony Express lasted only a little over one year when, with the advent of the telegraph system, it was slow and expensive by comparison.

The express was started by William Russell in the Autumn of 1859 in order to extend the business field of Russell, Majors and Waddell, the waggoners who supplied the Army posts. The best horses were purchased and the advertisements went up for...

'...Young, skinny and wiry fellows under 18 who are expert horsemen and willing to risk death daily. - Orphans preferred.'

The young Will Cody had already worked for the waggoners as a messenger and easily obtained a job in the new enterprise. It was here that he first met another youngster looking for adventure by the name of James Butler Hickok, who would leap into legend himself in later years with the more familiar name of 'Wild Bill'.

*The centre pages of the souvenir book illustrating the attack on the emmigrant train and rescue by Buffalo Bill.*

The first Pony Express rider left St. Joseph, Missouri at 5 p.m. on April 3rd, 1860. The destination was Sacramento, California and 75 horses would be needed to complete the ride, lasting ten and a half days. The cost for letters was ten dollars per ounce, but by October 1861 the telegraph had sealed the fate of the operation, with Russell losing $200,000. The event in the show would have had some sentimental value for Buffalo Bill and the Pony Express remained a part of the show until its end.

The programme next promised: 'ILLUSTRATES AN ATTACK on an Emigrant Train by the Indians and its Defence by Frontiersmen'. This was another of the set-pieces that the audiences seemed to appreciate most with plenty of horses and gunfire, and a happy ending. Into the arena would come the old Conestoga wagons, drawn by mules or horses and with outriders on their flanks. Sometimes, the children of visiting personalities were allowed to act the part of the settlers' children. The company would enact the end of a day's journey and the breaking of camp, with songs and laughter around the fires. This would be particularly effective during evening performances, and the Wells lamps hung around the arena would add to the tension of the audience. Over the years, the composition of this act was expanded from time to time with the addition of minor sub-acts such as cowboys riding broncs or the Virginia Reel danced by cowboys and western girls.

Suddenly, from the far side of the enclosure would come the Indians, their war-whoops resonating over the arena. The pioneers would take refuge behind the circled wagons, firing quickly before dropping back down to reload. As the painted warriors circled, the blue gunsmoke would begin to drift into the audience the smell of powder adding to the realism and excitement. Added to this were the shrieks of the women, the calls for more ammunition from the defenders and the constant thunder of hooves. Eventually, the Indians would penetrate the circle, shooting the defenders and taking hostages which they would duly tie to a stake. While some would be torturing the captives, the remainder of the Indians danced, until with a fanfare, and sometimes an introduction by the orator, Buffalo Bill would gallop in to save the whites. With him would be more scouts and cowboys. More firing and gunfire ensued as the battle turned into a multitude of individual combats, with the crowd shouting their advice and encouragement. During the 1892 season (possibly in England), Cody would himself pick up a young woman hostage and carry her out of the arena, seated on the horse behind him.

Following the blood and thunder of the Indian attack, or sometimes as part of the former event, came the Virginia Reel, danced on horseback by cowboys and 'prairie girls'. This probably served to change the tempo of the show but still hold the attention of the audience. Reports in the newspapers describe the performance as 'pretty', indicating also that the high-school horses were used. It is likely that during such slower sections, the vendors would walk the aisles selling souvenir programmes, drinks and candies.

The pace was quickened with the appearance of the Deadwood Stagecoach, pulled by six mules. Photographic evidence suggests that there may have been only four mules in early years. In the first visit to the UK in 1887, the coach was indeed the original. On the return voyage to the US aboard the Persian Monarch in 1888, during which it was lashed on deck, the coach suffered damage from the weather and a replacement was ordered by Cody.

*Programme illustration. Virginia reel on horseback.*

*Souvenir book illustration. Virginia reel on horseback.*

Members of the audience were permitted to ride the coach on occasion, with the orator charging the driver to take care of his 'precious cargo'. The cowboy band would play a Souza march and the vehicle would circle the arena to give the crowds a good look at the spectacle of a heavy vehicle pulled at speed by several pairs of mules, kicking up the dust on the bends. As if that were not enough, the excitement was heightened yet again with the entrance of another band of Sioux in hot pursuit of the coach. Once more, the cries of the attackers would rend the afternoon, accompanied by the reports from the rifles of the defenders of the mail. The distance between the Indians and the coach would gradually lessen until it looked as if there was no hope, and then, again in the 'nick of time', Buffalo Bill would ride in to save the day, with 'his attendant cowboys'. Cody would always lead the group, galloping after the retreating Indians, Colts and Winchesters blazing, in the true tradition of the Wild West, but not perhaps quite true to historical fact. Sometimes, as the nature of the different sequences developed from season to season, the attackers would not be Indians, but outlaws.

After the attack on the Deadwood Stagecoach, the excitement was maintained with a scene that became known as 'Cowboy Fun', in which traditional western horsemanship was demonstrated. The crowds always loved the bucking broncs, the riding and roping of wild buffalo, and in early years, the riding of an elk by a Negro cowboy . He was billed as 'An Indian from Africa'. Some reports state that cowboys were seldom thrown from their mounts, perhaps showing us that after many weeks of 'two performances daily', the horses became less enthusiastic in their efforts to unseat their riders. There are, however, other reports of Buffalo Bill bringing fresh horses over from America at the beginning of a new season, presumably for this reason.

One of the personalities in the show, an all-rounder who showed his expert handling of horses, was Buck Taylor, a six foot, five inch giant with an amiable disposition who was known on the billing as 'King of the Cowboys'. With his long hair, moustache and good looks, he was the very picture of the romantic, free-spirit of the plains. Taylor was with the show from the beginning, initially sporting a 'Buffalo Bill' goatee beard but later changing to a more fashionable moustache. Thrilling as the Wild West's scenes were of the life of the cowboy, little was mentioned in the performances of the hours of boredom, loneliness, fatigue and frostbite, and their sore-handed,

*Programme photographs showing the Deadwood stagecoach and inset how the photograph was used as a model for a postcard with the artist adding the grandstand behind.*

back-breaking hours in the saddle. The programmes did, however, sometimes make reference to the hardships of the cowboy.

A quieter period again ensued, with 'Life Customs of the Indians'. This portrayed a group moving on to a new campsite carrying their belongings by travois, a system of two poles dragged by a horse with a hide platform slung between them which supported the load. On reaching fresh ground, teepees were erected and the Indians settled down for the apparent night.

As the tableau unfolded with the Indians going about their everyday activities, there was a sudden attack by hostiles, the two tribes engaging in hand to hand combat with tomahawk and lance. Eventually, the invaders were driven off and the camp celebrated with 'Indian Feather Dances'. The significance, especially amongst British audiences, was sometimes lost, and often, the audiences were more amused than awed by the ritual...

'Then followed the Indian feather dance - fantastic, weird and grim it appears, but intensely amusing to those with the rhythm of the waltz.' (The Leicester Journal, Friday September 4th 1891.)

There was no pause, and as the last of the Indians left the arena, an increasing rumble heralded the beginning of the 'Wild Buffalo Hunt, featuring the last of the wild herds'. This last statement in the programme was not quite true, even though it was a fact that the bison still only existed in a few small pockets, where it was at last protected by Government decree.

Buffalo Bill would ride into the arena and dismount at a small, mock waterhole, allowing his horse to drink from water scooped up in his hat. As he mounted and rode off to one side, the canvas curtain would pull back to allow the small herd of twenty or so animals to enter at the gallop. Led usually by a big bull, there were also cows and calves, some never having seen the prairie, born into the captivity of the show business while the Wild West was on tour. As the impact of the buffalo settled over the crowd, Buffalo Bill, together with 'friendly' Indians or cowboys, would

gallop after them firing blanks and cutting out an animal, here and there, in demonstration of a hunt.

Although Cody's treatment of his stock was admirable by standards of the period, such treatment today would be rightly condemned. Recently discovered movie footage of this event, on the other hand, does not show the animals particularly stressed, as might be imagined. Perhaps, like the bucking horses, the weeks of regular performances made them used to the routine.

Some might wonder how Cody could take any pride in the scenes of the buffalo hunt, an event which, after all, helped to bring the species to the edge of extinction. It must be remembered that for much of his hunting career Cody killed buffalo for meat for the railroad workers, and the true nemesis for the bison were those who slaughtered for other reasons.

To control the plains Indians, the Government had encouraged the killing of the buffalo. The animals were killed in the hundreds of thousands for hides and also tongues, the latter becoming a delicacy in eastern cities for a time. Carcasses often littered the prairie, minus only their tongues which sold for just a few cents. Cody, to his credit, showed the hunt as it was practised by the Indians, from the back of a horse, and not like other professional hunters who, sitting nearly a mile distant, picked off the animals at their leisure with Sharps rifles. The outer animals were killed first until whole herds could be destroyed, the bison unable to hear the gunshots from so far away. This was known as a 'buffalo stand'. Some also believe that Cody's claims regarding the number of animals he killed were exaggerated. Be that as it may, happily these magnificent animals are still surviving in good numbers in places such as the Yellowstone and Custer National Parks in Wyoming and Dakota, and the National Buffalo Ranges in Montana. The wild without the buffalo is unimaginable.

As the afternoon progressed, 'An attack on a settler's cabin by Indians and Rescue by Buffalo Bill with his scouts, cowboys and Mexicans' was next on the programme. At the end of the arena, near the backdrop, a mock up of a small settlement was erected, complete with deer carcass and well. The settler (on occasion, John Y. Nelson), would bring in the horses for the night, with his son. While the animals were being bedded down, the settler's wife would be busying herself around the cabin, with washing and the like. As they worked, a war party would be seen creeping up with obvious intent on mischief. The Indians would be spotted and an exchange of shots would follow before, to save the day once more, along came Buffalo Bill and his retinue to drive off the hostiles.

The final act was the gathering of the whole of the Wild West before the delighted audience. In a similar format to the Grand Revue at the beginning, Buffalo Bill thanked those who had paid the price of admission, and said goodbye before inviting them to all to visit the encampment before going home. Who could have dismissed such an invitation? The camp must have been crowded with those wishing to say, in years to come, that they had visited Buffalo Bill's' camp and met Red Shirt, the notorious Indian Chief, in the flesh.

## Toward the 20th Century...

In 1892, the Wild West added 'Cossacks of the Caucasus' to the programme. This was the beginning of a much more varied show, becoming 'BUFFALO BILL'S WILD WEST AND CONGRESS OF ROUGH RIDERS OF THE WORLD'. Although still essentially based on equestrian events, it was expanded to include items which had little to do with a western theme. It seemed that the management, Cody and Salsbury, considered that, providing an act was authentic and exciting, it was worthy of inclusion. By 1904, during the Wild West's final tour of the UK, such events as the Cowboy Cyclist, and a demonstration by the US Life-Saving Service using breach apparatus were part of the show. Some of the epic, set-piece battle sequences were also allowed to stray from the western theme. Included from time to time were topical scenarios, such as scenes from the Spanish-American War and the Boxer rebellion of China. Such tried and proven attractions as the Attack on the Deadwood Stagecoach and the Pony Express, however, remained standard for the thirty year duration of the Wild West.

*Programme photograph. Cossacks of the Caucasus.*

1—The frontier hut—bringing home game.   2—Indians attacking frontier hut

*Souvenir book illustration.*

Also included by 1903 were displays by cavalry of various nationalities. Besides the Cossacks, here would be found British Lancers, American Frontier Cavalry, Arabs in flowing garb, Gauchos from Argentina, Mexican Ruralies, Japanese Mounted Samurai, Cuban Patriots, Roosevelt's Rough Riders and an American Artillery Battery giving its own demonstration of gun drill using an old style muzzle loader. There were close order foot drills by Zouaves, (soldiers of French-American descent), and Arab acrobats, all described in the newspaper advertisements as 'virile, martial manhood'.

The cowboy cyclist, it seems, was included for the 1904 season. This was an odd act in which the cyclist descended a curved ramp to pick up speed, and using the momentum, leapt a gap to land on another ramp some distance away. It was similar to the kind of activity that Evel Knievel would present on a motorcycle decades later. The distance of the gap varied from report to report, but was somewhere between forty and sixty feet. While the programme stressed that the act would not be included in the advent of high winds or heavy rain, such times were few. The only real western connection with the cyclist was that he wore a cowboy outfit. He was billed as 'Carter the Cowboy Cyclist', but it eventually became known by reporters of the time that, at least for some performances, he was someone by the name of George Davis. It is likely that due to the possibility of incapacity or accident, there would be more than one person who could perform the trick, and accidents certainly did happen. When the bicycle left the first ramp, a cannon was fired automatically as he sailed through the air, belching smoke to intensify the significance of the jump.

*Carter the Cowboy cyclist and his daring leap. Photograph from the 'Rough Rider' paper sold on the showground.*

Another rather odd event was the Life Saving Drill, again probably included for the 1904 season, as the newspaper advertisements for 1903 have no mention of either this feature or the cyclist. They may have been staged previously on the continent or in the US as posters showing these acts do exist circa 1901. At this time, teams of men, financed by the US Treasury Department, were stationed at notorious points around the American coastline to assist vessels in distress. For the purpose of the Wild West, the demonstration consisted of the transfer of 'survivors' from a mock-up of a mast, complete with crow's nest, in the centre of the arena. Posters which featured the event were given a degree of artistic license, showing a storm-tossed ship lurching badly in towering seas with the oilskin clad life-savers firing a hawser and preparing to row out to the stricken vessel. In the arena they would wear a naval style uniform with neat, peaked caps.

At the beginning of the demonstration the eight man team would march in with a beach cart containing the equipment. This was a simple two wheel vehicle similar to a caisson, the ammunition holder of a horse-drawn field gun. The life savers pulled the cart in two sections, by hand with ropes. While one section of men raised a simple frame known as the 'crotch', the other fired a hawser out to the unfortunate survivors clinging to the mast, by means of a small cannon. The hawser was then passed over the crotch and a breeches buoy installed, and by means of another rope it was pulled over to the mast, thereby giving a means of evacuation for the survivors. The equipment was then dismantled and neatly stowed. The whole crew would then march smartly away to the applause of the crowd. Although this event was patriotically appreciated by American audiences, it was also well received in the United Kingdom, being also a maritime nation. The Life Savers, of course, eventually became the US Coastguard.

Equestrian races of various kinds were part of the show over the years, the standard being a quarter mile dash between riders of differing origins. In earlier seasons, the main protagonists were cowboys, Indians and Mexicans, but as the Wild West developed, sometimes Arabs and Cossacks were included. The mounts used were suggested as being those naturally used by their riders, Indians for example, always riding paints or pintos, cowboys had their range ponies and Mexicans had their horses of Spanish decent. In fact, as it was originally the Spanish who brought the horse to North America, it could be argued that there was little difference in the distant pedigrees of many of the animals used in the Wild West. Of course, each group would have its own individual type of horse furniture to contrast and enhance each rider's individuality. Mexicans had large, high pommels to their saddles and winged stirrups, Arabs had ornate leatherwork, cowboys had more functional rigs and the Indians needed hardly anything other than a rein looped around the lower jaw of their mount. The title of the races changed over the life of the show, 'The International Race', 'The Grand Quarter Mile' and 'Race of Races'.

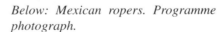

*Right: Oropeza, leader of the Mexicans and champion roper.*

*Below: Mexican ropers. Programme photograph.*

Other events on a similar theme included horse races between western girls and bareback riding and hurdling between Indian boys. There were also high school horses ridden by lady riders, such as Emma Lake Thatcher, a step-daughter of Wild Bill Hickok. She was billed as 'Emma Hickok - Champion equestrienne of the World', to capitalise on the name of her illustrious relative. Her mother, Agnes, had married Wild Bill five months prior to his murder - in the Number 10 saloon in Deadwood during a card game, by the infamous Jack McCall.

A novelty race was staged where an Indian on foot was matched against another who was mounted. The course was given several curves, where the rider would need to rein in considerably, giving the runner a distinct advantage and usually allowing him to win. Sometimes, the hundred yard course was run between two posts, fifty yards apart, the short distance and turn again countering the speed of the horse. There were also comic events to punctuate the main elements in the show, such as races using donkeys, relay races and clowns. The Wild West clowns should not be under-rated because of their comic overtones. In fact they were an important link between events, helping to maintain continuity and entertaining the audience before the commencement of the main programme. During some of the more dangerous sections, such as the bronc riding, they were invaluable as safety factors, keeping downed riders from being pummelled by the hooves of their mounts. Modern Rodeos have clowns which serve exactly the same purpose. Of all of the factors in the Wild West the clowns were seldom referred to as part of the show by the newspapers, and certainly hardly ever while the show was in the UK. They operated (usually) in pairs with names such as 'Timothy and Samanthy Hayseed', and 'Hidalgo', who wore a large sombrero and long-haired chaps, and rode a tiny donkey.

Season after season, different nationalities were represented in the arena with their own act, depicting their own particular skills. The Mexicans in the early years were led by Antonio Esquivel, a master horseman who commanded a prominent place in the billing. Another Mexican was the amazing Vicenti Oropeza, supremo with the lariat who could rope a breast of four horses, and many other feats. Oropeza, one time champion roper of Mexico, was very much respected and had previously served his country in the Grand Fiscal, a civilian police force organisation similar to the Texas Rangers. Joining the Wild West around 1894, he later passed on his skills to the famous film cowboy, Will Rogers. Severian Gonzales had served as Horse Master to the Mexican minister for war. The programme introduced this group as 'Vaqueros of the Southwest', explaining that there was little difference between their way of life and that of the American cowboy. In lurid style, it goes on to say...

"Your general vaquero, however, is generally, when off duty, more of a dandy in the style and get up of his attire than his careless and impetuous com-peer (the cowboy)".

Although performing a similar role to the cowboy, the Mexican's everyday costume and horse furniture was indeed generally much more flamboyant, with an obvious Spanish influence. The Mexicans in the Wild West, like most other performers, dressed for the appreciation of the audience in a certain amount of finery, with their jingling spurs, wide, sugar loaf sombreros and trimmed saddles.

Another favourite of the audiences, and Queen Victoria, were the Cossacks. They were the first non-western event of any substance to be included in the show, the first group of ten appearing in England in 1892. Over the years, the members of the group changed, some staying for just one season, and while billed as Cossacks, may have been Caucasian Jews or Georgians. Whatever their origin, they were Russian and brilliant horsemen, conforming to Buffalo Bill's idea that everything was genuine. Like other cultural groups, the Cossacks did not seem to be out of place in the Wild West, linked by being the symbolic horsemen of their country, like the Indians. Some were as young as eighteen, selected from their homeland by Cody's agents, C.M. Ercole and Joe Hart. An early leader of the Cossacks was Prince Ivan Rostamov Makharadse, said to be a descendant of Mazzepa, head of the Zaporogian clan and a Prince of the Ukraine, who history stated had fought their traditional enemies, the Turks and the Poles. Another leader of the Wild West's Cossacks was named Prince Soucca, who laid claim to the same lineage, so perhaps this title was just a part of Major Burke's programme hype. However, even if this were so, no one could doubt the skill and ability of the Russian horsemen.

At the beginning of their act the Cossacks would charge into the arena, sabres drawn, singing a battle hymn. Much of the event consisted of amazing feats of riding, one man standing on his head in the saddle while his horse ran at full gallop. Others swung from their mounts to pick up objects from the ground, then turning to ride on, sitting backwards in the saddle. There would also be national dances over swords, on a raised wooden platform, a game of tag on horseback and finally they would leave the arena with a full charge from the far end.

Their dress, some thought similar to a full dressing gown tied with a sash at the waist, but given a more military look by the addition of cartridge loops on each breast. On their heads, they wore the traditional soft fur hats and the trousers, just visible between the coat and supple, knee-high boots, were baggy. They carried curved swords in scabbards, daggers, pistols and rifles. The 1906 programme explains how the Cossacks were historically matched against lancers, becoming the world's greatest swordsmen as they learned to dodge between the long, lethal spikes.

Another non-western group were the Gauchos from the Pamapas of South America, first appearing in the 1894 season at Ambrose Park, Brooklyn. These equally skilful riders from Argentina filled the role of stockmen, like their counterparts from North America. Like the cowboys and Mexicans, they used the lasso to great effect but were also devastatingly accurate with the bolas. The bolas was a trio of thin ropes joined at one point with each free end having a weight attached, the idea being to throw it to entangle an animal by the legs and bring it down. In their act in the show the Gauchos used two poles to demonstrate their skill, rather than live animals. They also showed their ability with horses, roping and riding wild broncos.

Like the other cultural groups the Gauchos appeared on several of the posters as part of the Congress of Rough Riders, but at least two from 1896 and 1899 featured them alone. These beautiful examples of the art of the period are by the Courier Lithographic Company of Buffalo and are part of a series of one-sheet bills (28" x 42") depicting each individual group in the Wild West. The 1896 poster shows the Gauchos chasing llamas with their bolas, but it is uncertain as to whether these animals were actually part of the show.

The Gauchos wore pill box hats with several pom-poms attached to them, full shirts and even fuller riding breeches which were gathered into their boots. They had large spurs and carried their bolas tied around their waists. The horse furniture, like the Cossacks, was quite simple but one or two had ornately carved, wooden, full-foot stirrups.

By 1899 a group of Arab horsemen were included in the Wild West, billed as 'Real Sons of the Soudan' (sic), and 'Riffian Arab Horsemen from Morocco'. In the manner of the other groups, the Arabs performed brilliant horse acrobatics but also brought their own particular skills, such as the spinning and throwing of their ornate flintlock muskets. At the gallop , there was much sword clashing and twirling, and gunfire. With the horsemen were tumblers who transformed themselves into human pyramids, tightrope walkers and other acrobatic feats to the accompaniment of thundering hooves.

The Arabs were one the most colourful of the ethnic groups with their flowing robes, magnificent horses and elaborate saddles and bridles. The group of Japanese Samurai were sometimes seen as being very similar. English audiences especially were inclined to appreciate the Samurai less than the other groups but it must be remembered that Japan had opened its borders to the outside world only a few years before, and little at the time was known by the average man of its history or culture.

As the years progressed, more military kinds of equestrian events were included. Where once the various nationalities had their own events, they eventually became grouped together under various titles such as 'Ten Minutes with the Rough Riders of the World'. While the show was in England, this changed to 'Exhibitions of Seats in the Saddle'. The expansion of the Wild West's equestrian composition is probably what Nate Salsbury had envisaged from his first involvement with the show, and it cannot be denied that the variety of acts, although selected carefully to conform, did still draw the crowds at both home and foreign venues.

*Arab acrobats. Programme photograph.*

*Composite photograph from the programme showing US Cavalry drill.*

32

So by the end of 1892, the Wild West advertised English Lancers, German Uhlans, French Chasseurs and contingents of the Sixth United States Cavalry. Most were retired or reserve soldiers but some were given special dispensation to appear with the show, and many had seen action in the uniform that they wore in the Wild West. These troops would also take part in the opening and final revues, and even more than the ethnic riders, the military contingents gave definite signals of race, nationality and ability by their distinctive uniforms. Many had won honours for their country and these were sometimes announced within the context of the performances. Later, as the century waned and war with Spain loomed, further pride in the American forces was invited with the addition of Thorpe's Battery, Fifth United States Artillery. The battery was often applauded as its horses hauled their guns and caissons over the rough ground, and gave a demonstration of servicing the muzzle loaders. Over the years, several gunners lost an arm due to premature ignition while loading the cannons. Later still, Grime's' Battery would demonstrate its part in the taking of San Juan Hill, perhaps the most famous of the engagements of the Spanish-American War in Cuba.

*Programme photograph of a contingent of Roosevelt's Rough Riders*

At the end of 1893, the sheer variety of the ethnic and military riders was impressive. A group of Filipino Insurgents was added, a contingent of Puerto Ricans, Cuban Patriots and a detachment of Hungarian Ciskos, but many of the riders would change uniform for the battle scenes, to become Spaniards or Chinese.

Like the national groups, military riders showed their own particular skills. English lancers gave tent-pegging demonstrations, others sliced lemons at the gallop with sabres, all interspersed with cavalry manoeuvres. All would be in dress uniform for the best possible effect and with flying pennants, flashing sabres, dazzling colours and superb horses, the spectacle must have been hypnotic. Much was made of this dash and daring on the posters and advertising.

As a complete alternative to the horse soldiers, a company of Aurora Zouaves gave a wonderful display of close order drill in double time, a half step to whistle commands. The uniform of these men was flamboyant in the extreme showing variations of French - Arab influence. They wore the fez, knee length, baggy pantaloons, sleeveless waistcoats and long, buttoned gaiters, magnificent in red and white. Originally organised as militia, the Zouaves had a long pedigree, fighting for the Union during the Civil War. This particular group was replaced by the Devlin

*Samurai swordsmen. Photograph from the 'Rough Rider'.*

Zouaves, and completed the event by scaling a sheer wall using only rifles and slings and each other's shoulders for supports.

Although the audiences appreciated the flash and daring of riders, races and military drill, it was the big, set-piece re-enactments which certainly gripped their imaginations. Like other sections in the show, these changed during the lifetime of the Wild West to take into account developing attitudes and interest of the audience to the world around them. In this way, some topical scenes were shown to reflect current conflicts such as the Spanish American War or the Boxer Rebellion in China. By the time such non western scenarios were included, ethnic groups of riders were already performing regularly and as the scenes usually involved American forces and horses, they were accepted as appropriate to the programme.

A Cavalry rider.

Some western sections were part of the show until the end and seldom changed in context, and only a little in expedition. These included the attack on the stagecoach and the Pony Express. Sometimes the titles changed. For example, the attack on the settler's cabin became 'Ranch Life in the West' by 1906.

The 'Attack on the Deadwood Stagecoach' was the act which more than any other epitomised the show, and changed least. It told a simple story, travellers attacked by Indians or bandits, and always rescued by Buffalo Bill and his 'attendant' cowboys and scouts. With the wagons, the coach was one of the largest props used by the Wild West, and became quite battered by the regular, daily attacks as time wore on. Newspaper reports show that its condition was noticed and one programme states...

"As it now stands, the leather binds of the windows are worn, the paint is now faded, and it has a battered and travel stained aspect that tells the story of hardship and adventure."

From this we might deduce that little was done to keep the coach in pristine condition, presumably the idea being that its beaten countenance added to the authenticity.

The stagecoach, the Pony Express and the buffalo hunt, the simplest of the re-enactments, had the least performers and are described elsewhere. In the big battle sequences, sometimes several hundred people and horses were in the arena at the same time. On one occasion it was suggested there were five hundred or more, but this is doubtful, for if that were the case it must have included ticket sellers, chefs and other denizens of the catering department. If a specific, central character was essential to the scene, then it was usually portrayed by Buffalo Bill, not least when the story revolved around one of his own exploits. One exception, however was the staging of 'Custer's Last Stand'. It was not conducive to the spirit of the show for the audience to see the star defeated, and so for some time, Custer was played by Buck Taylor. Buffalo Bill would enter the scene after the battle and the demise of the cavalry, appearing as himself, too late to save the day. This of course, is historically incorrect but allowed Cody to be involved for the purposes of

*Programme illustration which shows an artists impression of the charge at San Juan Hill. In the foreground is Grime's Battery.*

*Above Right: Standard advertising block used in newspaper advertisements.*

the show and perhaps suggested to onlookers that had he been there, the outcome may well have been different. Cody had known Custer well, hunting with him many times, not least when guiding the Grand Duke Alexis on his visit to the west.

In all, during the life of the show, sixteen different set-pieces were staged and basically these fell into two categories, the general tableaux such as the attack on the emigrant train, and those depicting actual events. The battle scenes were the longest, lasting between fifteen and twenty minutes to complete. Some were quite complicated to stage where it was necessary to follow a historical storyline, and in many of these scenarios, individuals, and certainly military units, who were involved in

the real events were featured to add to the authenticity. Over the years, six large, battle sequences were included in the programme.

Buffalo Bill's duel with Yellow Hand (Yellow Hair) is also described elsewhere. This scene was staged while the show was in England but was dropped after two seasons. While audiences accepted the clinical demise of an enemy from a bullet, it has been said that they were unhappy to see Cody take the Indian's scalp, to English crowds a most un-gentlemanly thing to do. Unlike today's mass audiences, those who watched the Wild West's enactments were still sensitive to explicit violence at close hand. The duel was acted out with much exaggeration as can be seen at the end of Robert Altman's excellent (if somewhat jaundiced) film, 'Buffalo Bill and the Indians'.

In 1886, at Madison Square Garden, 'Custer's Last Battle', or the 'Battle of the Little Bighorn', was introduced. The battle remained a part of the show on all visits to the UK, being changed in 1907 for another similar scene, 'The Battle of Summit Springs'. Two things were different about this new scene, one being the direct involvement of Buffalo Bill in the actual event and the other being that in this one, the Indians were beaten.

The battle sequences usually had two phases, one to set the scene and the other the actual fight. Custer's downfall (on the 27th June 1876) was no exception. The first part was prone to be occasionally changed. Originally it showed the cavalry breaking camp during the early morning, then saddling up and moving out to find the Indians. Later it was changed to an opposite view, showing the Indians in their camp, complete with teepees, dogs and squaws. There would be a war dance and during this, a scout would be seen by the audience to reconnoitre for a while before riding off. To the sound of the cowboy band playing Custer's favourite marching song, 'Gary Owen', the cavalry would charge in (usually on white horses), and the battle joined. Much gunfire, smoke and individual combats ensued, with Buck Taylor, as Custer, being the last to fall. The Indians would then carry off their wounded and break camp. From a different direction, Buffalo Bill would enter with his group of scouts and cowboys. They would survey the scene and display mourning for the fallen. Sometimes, especially during evening performances where it was more dramatic, a spotlight would pick out Cody, standing with hung head, and a sign would be lit up displaying the words, 'TOO LATE'.

Of course, little of the involvement of Cody in the above was accurate, but the general aspect of the scene was. Cody had no way of including the Americans who took part in the battle, but some of the Sioux in the show, including some of the women, were reported to have taken part in the battle and the aftermath. There are conflicting accounts of whether Sitting Bull actually took part in the fighting. Being more of a Holy man than a War Chief, it is more likely he would have been kept informed of events as they happened and probably took more part in an advisory role. The battle itself, like many such incidents, has been blown up into monumental proportions. Historians agree that Custer's splitting of his command was his downfall. Some of the 225 cavalrymen who died at the Little Bighorn, it now seems, were raw recruits, some hardly ever having used their carbines. The conflict itself probably lasted little more than a half hour, a brief engagement by unhorsed regular cavalry fighting their way up a hillside to higher ground. According to unconfirmed Indian accounts, Custer, well known to the Sioux and an obvious target, was among the first to fall. A different picture to the usual Hollywood version where the gallant buck-skinned commander stands alone on a hillock, surrounded by his fallen comrades, sabre in hand.

The re-enactment of the Summit Springs engagement was very similar to the Custer battle, given added interest with the inclusion of white female hostages, some of whom were tortured by the Indians. This actually happened, one killed and the other apparently rescued by Cody in real life. In the show, Cody was the scout that discovered the camp and returned with the cavalry, and was close to the actual events. As the horsemen came to the rescue they demolished the teepees and drove off the Indians, then leaving the arena in triumph. A little while later the Indians returned to recover what was left of their camp, making the clearing of the arena for the next act as part of the performance, and maintaining the audience's interest.

In 1898, American troops were engaged in the war against the Spanish in Cuba. National patriotism was high, and it was natural that the Wild West soon included aspects of the conflict within its programme. A contingent of sixteen of Roosevelt's Rough Riders was included, together with eight Cubans, three Filipinos and seven Hawaiians, some of whom crossed the Atlantic with Buffalo Bill on the European tour of 1902-4. Roosevelt had coined the term 'Rough Rider' from the Wild West, Cody first using the term in 1892. No doubt he was happy for it to be used in his country's interest. The unit's proper title was the First Regiment, United States Volunteer Cavalry and was drawn from professional horsemen such as cowboys and reserve cavalrymen. Some of the cast of the Wild West left to fight in the war and returned after the Spanish were beaten.

Also on the bill for these seasons was the 'Battle for San Juan Hill', a non-western scenario based upon the famous incident in which Teddy Roosevelt led his khaki clad (dismounted) cavalry against a heavily fortified blockhouse, held by entrenched and more numerous Spanish, equipped with Mausers. As already mentioned, some of these actual participants joined the Wild West to re-enact the event. Another veteran group from the action was Grime's Battery, who had operated Gattling guns in support of the heroic charge. Other units represented included the 71st Infantry, Cuban Scouts and the mule pack train.

Again, the scene was organised into two sections. The first showed the setting up of camp on the eve of the battle; picketing of horses and mules. Campfire songs were sung and sentries put out. After a pause, to simulate the passing of night, reveille aroused the camp and signalled the beginning of the second part, situated at the fork of a road, at the foot of San Juan Hill. To the strains of ' A hot time in the old town tonight', the column advanced toward the blockhouse, breastworks and rifle pits, all shown to illustrate the huge task of the American forces. Colonel Theodore Roosevelt, of course played by Buffalo Bill, then pressed forward, calling for his men to follow the flag. It was suggested in the programme that the Spanish could not believe that such a small force was seriously attacking such a strong position, and that a larger one was pressing forward in the smoke behind them. This may have been true. Whatever the case, the Americans won the day, both in history and in the retelling in the Wild West. The final stages of the performance showed hand to hand fighting between the two sides (the Spanish played by Indians and other members of the cast), the retreat and tearing down of the Spanish flag. Lastly, the Stars and Bars, 'Old Glory', the American flag was raised and seen fluttering atop a flagpole, and the battle was over.

The other blatantly non western conflict staged was the Battle of Tien-Tsin. In 1900, Chinese Boxer rebels attacked the diplomatic compound at Peking, besieging the occupants and a small multinational force of soldiers and diplomats. After holding out for a considerable period, a relief force sent by several nations arrived to drive off the Boxers and ultimately put an end to the Royal dynasties.

The display again was staged in two parts, loosely based upon the rescue of the diplomats. In the first, the 'Assembly of the Powers' is depicted with the inevitable drills and manoeuvres of each participating detachment. When this was completed the columns moved off to advance upon Tien-Tsin. In the second segment the soldiers were at the gates of the city, which lay beyond a simulated moat, and these were subsequently stormed and secured by the allied forces. In this event the Chinese were played by Indians, but many of the soldiers in the rescuing regiments actually took part in the real thing. They included Japanese, German, Russian, French, Sikhs, British and US Marines, Welsh Fusiliers and the Ninth US Infantry, all carrying their regimental colours. It is interesting to note that the description of the event in the programme admits to artistic license being used, 'in the interest of making the display more interesting to the public'.

Reference was also made in the Wild West to the Boer War while this remained topical to the audiences, a troop of British horsemen representing a particular regiment.

There were, in the thirty years of the Wild West, several other types of dramatic tableau presented apart from those described here. Some were successful and remained for many seasons, while others not so well received were quickly dropped. One of the latter, known as 'The Horse Thief', would be considered barbaric even today. This event appeared in the programme during the last great tour of the UK in 1903/4. A lone cowboy was seen to bed his horse down for a night on the prairie, and after he was seen to 'graphically' fall asleep, another rider (the horse thief) would creep up and steal the horse. When the owner awoke and discovered his loss, a detachment of cavalry and scouts would appear and after brief discussion, would take off in pursuit of the bandit. Needless to say, the thief was caught, and there followed a series of very unpleasant (for the thief) punishments. These included feigned brutality. It must be remembered that a man afoot in the badlands of the south-west was in dire straits indeed, and the usual end for a horse thief, when caught, was immediate lynching. The Wild West thief was roped and dragged for a considerable distance behind a horse, while other riders fired off pistols at his struggling body. Reports in Yorkshire and Lincolnshire papers show that British audiences enjoyed the act but in America it was considered too violent, especially for women and children. It was dropped from the show.

An unusual inclusion in later years was an act entitled 'The Far East', or 'A Dream of the Orient'. As its title suggests, the display was loosely based on an Arabian Nights theme with exotic animals, Sheikhs and acrobats. There was a story line in which Europeans were captured and entertained during their imprisonment by Arabs, while a ransom was paid. The end came with the arrival of the money and release of the captives. It was a rather strange scene, probably staged to make good use of all of the eastern national groups employed by the Wild West. This event was included after the involvement of Pawnee Bill, who eventually merged his show with the Wild West, as described later.

*Programme photograph. Roping a bucking Horse.*

In 1907 and 1908, after the deaths of Nate Salsbury and James Bailey, and prior to his partnership with Pawnee Bill, Cody made a determined effort to steer the Wild West away from the circus influence introduced by Bailey and back to its original form. He introduced the 'Great Train Hold-up'. Bandits would stop the train and uncouple the engine, then proceed to rob the express car and the passengers. As they dynamited the safe, the Union Pacific Railroad's agents, led by Buffalo Bill, would appear and eventually capture the bandits. The train was a scaled down version of the real thing, moved by clever use of an automobile, but was apparently very true to detail. Individuals from the audience were sometimes invited to play the part of the passengers, first being taken behind the scenes to board. Occasionally, the robber band was led by a woman to add interest, and also to show that while most frontier women were wholesome, one or two sometimes went astray.

Although briefly described in another section, 'cowboy fun' deserves a little more explanation. This was the most accurate western section of the show, depicting more honestly the everyday routine of the cowboy and his environment. Like the rest of the acts in the Wild West, it was prone to change over the seasons, sometimes becoming part of other scenarios or enlarged in its own right with the addition of ethnic groups of stockmen, like the Gauchos. In the arena the cowboys had to deal with bucking horses, rope and herd wild Texas cattle and even ride and throw buffalo. The bulk of the act revolved around skill with horses, and included fancy riding and picking up objects from the ground at the gallop. Audiences world-wide enjoyed the saddle bronc riding, which was the most thrilling part of the act. Many of these horses had been the product of bad handling, and becoming vicious and unmanageable, were sold on for a reduced sum to Wild West shows such as Buffalo Bill's. For these horses, their treatment while with the Wild West was a great improvement on previous times. In the arena, it was usually the cowboys who came off worst. Consequently, the horses were given names to match their meanness, such as 'Texas Tornado' and 'Leatherbiter', and usually lived up to them. One active animal was known as 'Dynamite', due to his particularly explosive nature. Cowboys had to rope and hold the horses long

*Programme illustration. Cowboy Fun.*

enough for the rider to mount, a process known as 'snubbing'. Sometimes the horse was thrown onto its side, allowing the cowboy to take the saddle from this position, but the thrashing of the animal as it regained its feet could give the rider real problems. Many injuries occurred. Once up and away there was no easy way to dismount and participants either rode the horse until it tired or were thrown off. Women riders were also part of the event during most seasons.

*Programme photograph. Saddling a bucking horse.*

Inevitably some horses would eventually become used to the weight on their backs and so a device called a bucking strap was sometimes used. This was a leather band fastened around the horse's belly that would irritate it into bucking for a short period. The Wild West denied the use of this device but it is more likely that it was used. At the beginning of each season, fresh horses were usually introduced or shipped if the show was abroad.

Some cowboys' speciality was the roping and throwing of wild Texas steers, much as happens in modern rodeos, but these animals were the long horned cattle once herded by the Spanish around the Rio Grande, which had escaped and gone as wild as the buffalo. Their stamina and hardiness was legendary and were sometimes interbred with domestic stock, giving the best of qualities to the calves. In this way, domestic cattle could better endure the long drives which would eventually lead to the eastern

markets. The roping and riding of wild buffalo was similar in most respects, except for the unfamiliarity of the audiences with the animals, making the event more unusual. Some of the big bulls could be particularly difficult because of their weight, and Buffalo Bill was once hospitalised for two weeks after attempting to ride such an animal after others had refused.

So far, we have discussed the Wild West as a travelling show, but there were times when, both in the UK and the US, it remained in one place for a considerable time, allowing the use of more spectacular effects. This happened for the first time in 1886 when Steel MacKaye, playwright and theatrical producer, was introduced to Cody and Salsbury, and seeing the potential of the show, arranged for the Wild West to play at Madison Square Garden in a rolling tableau which they named 'The Drama of Civilisation'.

Matthew Morgan was a painter who had worked upon huge dioramas in St. Louis, depicting the Civil War. In all, twelve giant paintings, 45 feet by 27 feet high, had been completed, making Morgan the ideal candidate to produce the great backdrops required to reflect the rolling prairies, rivers and mountains for the Wild West. Said to have cost $40,000, these backdrops would be forty feet high, and a monumental task for the artist, working from a swinging chair. The scenes could be changed by means of revolving drums and the arena was carpeted with bark chips. Flags of all nations were flown from the rafters.

*Cowboys of Buffalo Bill's Wild West. Programme Photograph.*

The opening was set for November 27th, and invited were Generals Sherman and Sheridan, and also Custer's widow, Elizabeth Bacon Custer. As the lights faded, Cody's voice welcomed those attending. Spotlights then picked out groups of riders entering the arena, Indians, Mexicans, and finally, Buffalo Bill riding 'Old Charlie'.

After the opening revue, the arena cleared and a simulated sunrise revealed a forest, complete with animals, and in a small clearing, an Indian encampment. As a dance began, the camp was attacked by a hostile tribe and battle ensued as the lights dimmed. Next came Annie Oakley with her shooting act, then the attack on the immigrant train by Indians. The attack repulsed, the wagons then had to flee from a prairie fire, along with elk and buffalo. Then followed the Virginia Reel performed on horseback, with vignettes of cowboy life on the perimeter. As the display progressed, Indians could be seen creeping into the scene, eventually attacking and taking prisoners. These were then rescued by Buffalo Bill and his scouts and frontiersmen. Johnny Baker then entertained the audience with more sharpshooting while Mexicans displayed their skills with the rope.

The cowboy band then played 'Gary Owen', to introduce the next section, 'Custer's Last Stand', with Buck Taylor as the unfortunate general. The scene progressed in the manner already described.

Then came dancing by Indians, the grass dance, the rain dance, and the antelope dance, which faded into a view of a mining camp in the Rocky Mountains. Because of the venue, the scenery was much more elaborate than when the show was on the road, allowing the construction of hillsides and forests. The scene developed to show the Pony Express, and then the stagecoach entered. This was stopped by bandits, who cut free the mules, shot the passengers and made off with the strongbox. At this stage the effects really came into their own with the staging of a cyclone to complete the spectacle. MacKaye had hired a brilliant engineer, Nelse Waldron, to build the cyclone machinery. The effect was achieved by means of an underground wind tunnel leading into the building, and together with tents tearing loose, tumbleweed, fleeing animals and humans, must have been awe inspiring to spectators. Bags of dried leaves had been collected and were allowed to swirl in the windstorm, until finally the lights dimmed and calm again overshadowed the arena.

As the lights came up again, the whole cast was assembled, mounted, to take the final bow. The whole show was formulated to flow smoothly from one scene to another, depicting the frontier as the producers wished it to be seen. We can only marvel today at the ingenuity of such productions. The season was hailed as a winter triumph, finishing on February 22nd, 1887.

The more elaborate shows were possible while the Wild West performed at Earle's Court in 1887, and when it then moved on to Manchester in the autumn of that year, Cody and Salsbury had their own building erected to house the show and performers. Built on the race track at Salford, it was advertised as the 'largest living theatre in the world', heated by steam and lit by electricity, the arena itself large enough to give the illusion of perspective. The existing facilities of the race track were used to stable the livestock.

'The Avalanche' was another of the complicated spectacles staged when the show played its longer, static engagements. In 1908 it was performed at Madison Square Garden and depicted a mountain settlement during a snowstorm. The stagecoach was seen trying to fight its way back to town through worsening conditions, then overturning and causing the avalanche, which eventually destroyed the camp, burying the occupants. Sadly, little information survives to explain how the effect was achieved, and we must therefore trust to our imagination.

This then, was Buffalo Bill's Wild West in its many forms, but another aspect of the show, outside of its performances which is seldom discussed and rarely given the importance it deserves, is the street parade. For a greater part of its life, the Wild West was a travelling show regularly giving one day performances, then moving on to the next venue. As you will see in greater detail in other sections of this book, the show routinely rolled into town by train during the early morning, set up the ground, gave a parade through the streets around noon, then produced afternoon and evening performances before moving on to the next stand.

This was a costly exercise and therefore the Wild West had to attract as many people as possible within a limited time to visit the show. Of course, one way of doing this was by means of posters and advance newspaper advertisements, but nothing could possibly impress so many people on the day of the show than a parade of the most exciting elements of the Wild West. Many interesting stories evolved around the parades as they wound through the town centres, slowing and sometimes stopping commercial traffic.

*Mr. Sweeney's Cowboy Band. Programme photograph.*

As may be imagined, Buffalo Bill would head the column, usually followed by the band wagon from which would come stirring music. This would attract more people, who were out of direct view but within earshot. Behind the musicians would be troupes of Indians, cowboys and other riders, many carrying flags and banners. Also taking part was the Deadwood Stagecoach and covered wagons, mules and some of the bucking horses, which sometimes caused disturbances as they were led along the road and created even more good publicity for the show. As time progressed, the electricity generating machinery was included to convince audiences that the Wild West boasted every modern convenience for their benefit. Photographs still exist showing the generating wagon in the parades.

Streets would be lined with spectators and small boys would follow the parade, in later life telling their grandchildren about the event. Many would follow the riders right back to the showgrounds where they were able to wander around the perimeter, hoping to catch glimpses of the Indians. Some street urchins were lucky enough to be chosen to perform menial tasks for the show, and were paid quite handsomely. After the show, audiences were invited by Buffalo Bill to visit the camp where a further opportunity was created for the sale of souvenirs. Some of the Indians quickly found the advantage of selling 'personal' possessions to the visitors, while keeping a good stock of similar items out of sight in the teepees.

*A street parade showing Indians, Arabs and Lancers. The photograph was actually taken in Belgium.*

As town centres eventually became more congested with motor traffic, the parades were discontinued. Passing cars were known to hoot at the procession, occasionally causing horses to become too unmanageable, and an injury to the public would have been disastrous.

James Bailey's influence on the show, as we have seen, was evident with the inclusion of acts with a circus connotation, and also the addition of a concourse of side-shows which could be visited by the public prior to performances. Cody and Salsbury disliked this intensely, but were obliged to allow Bailey his way, consoled a little, no doubt, by the extra revenue created.

The acts used in the side-shows were varied and definitely circus. These included fire-eaters, snake charmers, jugglers, acrobats, a bearded lady and a mind reader. From the Wild West, Johnny Burke No-Neck (the four-year old found on the battlefield of Wounded Knee) was put on display, together with the wife and baby of Luther Standing Bear. John Y. Nelson was also persuaded to take to the boards with his Indian wife and numerous children. Nelson also played a role in the show as shotgun rider on the stagecoach and sometimes as the settler attacked by Indians.

While waiting for the show to begin, visitors could also inspect the livestock and listen to the cowboy band, which began playing half an hour before the beginning of each performance. Another attraction was the gyroscope, housed in its own tent. Again little is known about the attraction but it was probably similar to equipment used in UK fairs until quite recently, where a large revolving drum gradually forced participants outwards from the centre and up the walls, to be held there by centrifugal force. A more sophisticated version of this was also used later in the training of astronauts, helping accustom them to G forces.

In the US the Wild West employed detectives from the famous Pinkerton Agency to patrol the grounds and protect the public from the predation of thieves and pickpockets. Local constabularies also played their part while the show was on tour in the UK. The police also aided the flow of people and traffic to and from the show and on occasion helped with emergencies.

The programmes sold on the grounds give a great insight into the workings of the Wild West and certainly, this book would never have been written without access to such a publication. However, to solely rely upon the programme would be folly, as much of the text was written by Major Burke (Arizona John) in his exaggerated and florid fashion, in order to promote Buffalo Bill and his lifestyle for the financial benefit of those involved. Nate Salsbury disliked any exaggeration but went along with it for presumably the same reasons. Bearing this in mind, the quality and value for money of the booklets, some of which were well over sixty pages long, was excellent. For a few pennies the purchaser was treated to an account of the personal and public history of Buffalo Bill, combined with lessons in history and geography of the United States. While some of the detail may have been suspect, the presentation was superb and at times was produced in the shapes of Indian and buffalo heads. Always, the colourful front cover carried a portrait of Cody, surrounded by small vignettes of aspects of his life such as the Deadwood Stagecoach, Indians or a herd of buffalo. Inside the first pages would be a list of the various scenes in the show for that season, a brief explanation of each and an interesting warning to the public that read. . .

"Any demand for fees, the acceptance of money for seats by ushers or other employees, incivility or inattention of attaches, will not be tolerated. Patrons will confer a favour by reporting to the management any violation of this rule."

A note that we might still find refreshing today. The Wild West cared for its visitors, and with sentiments such as this, was seen to do so.

Also in the first pages were advertisements, which convey an interest in their own right for researchers. Of course, Buffalo Bill's autobiography 'Last of the Great Scouts', took pride of place, at the princely sum of two shillings and sixpence.

According to the programme, Dunn's famous hats were providing value and economy at three shillings and ninepence, and the 'Parisian' perambulator (a smart design in American Reed), could be obtained from Trotman's of Holloway Road, London - a steal at four pounds and four shillings, carriage paid. The British programmes advertised everything from Wright's Coal Tar Soap (fourpence) to products which could help alcoholic excess, and something named 'Vegox', a pure essence of fresh vegetables and prime ox beef. Spratt's bird and parrot foods were evident, ladies costumes (made to order) at two and a half guineas, and Pepper's Quinine and Iron Tonic for general disability.

There was a full page introduction, apparently penned by Nate Salsbury, but may have had the touch of Major Burke. It described in detail the many triumphs of the Wild West in its travels, including the visits of such personalities as Queen Victoria and many other Royal personages. The tone of the article was self-praising, and rightly so as nothing could have been so effective an ambassador for the United States as Buffalo Bill's Wild West. In some ways the introduction gives the impression that the writer was making the case for a return to Europe, but if this were so, it was certainly unnecessary, as the flow of visitors proved.

The next few pages returned to Burke's usual floral style and blatantly extolled the virtues of the hero of the show in all ways. The whole purpose seems to have been to show that there was no aspect of Cody's life that was not heroic, wholesome or spectacular. To add weight to this, included in the text were statements solicited by the press department, obtained from various high-ranking officers with whom Buffalo Bill had served as a scout. In truth, these officers had willingly complied, and agreed that Cody's service in this capacity had been excellent. In the tenth edition there was a full page illustration showing a portrait of Cody surrounded by pictures of the famous generals, with whom he had been involved during his career.

The programme text was generously salted with photographs and illustrations. Many of the photographs are obviously retouched for the benefit of clarity but the illustrations are beautifully stylised, much in the manner of the nineteenth century artists.

Some pictures are a mixture of both. For example, one shows a photograph of the Coliseum in Rome with drawings of Indians and teepees, added later and suggesting that this was a scene that the photographers missed. In most issues of the programme, the famous photograph of Buffalo Bill and Sitting Bull is included with the sub text, 'Foes in '76, Friends in '85'.

*Buffalo Bill and Sitting Bull. "foes in '76, friends in '85". Photograph reproduced from the programme.*

*Credit page from 10th edition of the programme.*

The picture was actually taken while the Wild West was in Montreal, Canada (1885) by the photographer William Notman. There are suggestions that this picture was copied (and copyrighted) by other photographers. For purchasers of the programme, many of whom would be familiar with the comic-like presentation of the dime novels, the photographs would give an added sense of authenticity to the proceedings, but this could be misleading. For instance, one full page shows several photographs of 'Historic Red Men', visually suggesting that they were, or had been, involved with Buffalo Bill and the Wild West, and two, Gall and Chief Joseph, certainly had not been.

Apart from Cody, many of the other star performers are featured in the text, explaining their backgrounds and the skills that the audience might expect to see in the show. Various aspects of the performances are explained, such as the importance of the Deadwood Stagecoach and the Virginia reel performed on horseback, and a large number of pages devoted to the various ethnic groups of riders. It is thanks to such documentation that we know the content of such acts as the Cossacks and the 'Attack on San Juan Hill'. Other interesting inclusions were articles such as 'The Passing of the Cowboy', a note on Roosevelt's Rough Riders and 'The Bucking Bronco'.

There were notes on the recent history of America including several pages on the various Indians, some of whom had been involved in the Ghost Dance uprising, which was also documented. In most of these articles, Burke managed to suggest that Buffalo Bill was either directly or indirectly involved, which was sometimes only partly correct. Much of Cody's private life was discussed, showing pictures of, and describing his ranch and hunting lodge, the town of Cody which he founded, and his various interests and prosperity. No doubt this was to reinforce the successes of the Wild West, and before the increasing interests of the Treasury Department.

The final pages of the programme relate to the European tours in greater detail. Here can be found interesting references to some of the ships which transported the show and especially for the purposes of this book, reference to tours of the UK too numerous to list. These items provide a pathway to research about the Wild West in greater detail.

*Major John M. Burke.*

Lastly, on page sixty-four of issue number ten is a final word from Major Burke entitled, 'The Home of History'. He explains the importance of the Wild West in recreating history for the audience, and its pedigree linked with bygone heroes such as Kit Carson and Daniel Boone, and of course the (then) living hero, Buffalo Bill. In short, the article summarises and reinforces the previous pages, and as if to prove his conviction, there is a small photograph of Burke, centrally placed. Facing this page was advice for those wishing to take advantage of railway excursions to the performances.

Because of the amount and variation of information included, the programmes are difficult to summarise in a few words. Suffice to say, today they are fascinating documents of a time long gone. Like the Wild West itself, they are interesting and unusual, sometimes factually wanting but always exciting, and still a part of history.

*Above: Cody's TE Ranch.*

*Below: Cody's Nebraska home, the 'Scout's Rest Ranch'.*

## WONDROUS WILD
## 1887/8

*'The first visit of the Wild West to England. Buffalo Bill in Hull. A final performance. Navigating the Humber by steamer. Sioux and Stowaways.'*

We have seen in the last section how the Wild West developed and eventually came to the shores of England for the American Exhibition of 1887. Cody took London by storm and even the orator, Frank Richmond, gained appreciation from Queen Victoria for his 'very pleasant description of the Wild West'. The Dowager Marchioness of Ely was instructed by the Queen to find a suitable gift to bestow on Richmond for his inspiring oration, and a Parian marble bust of the Sovereign was deemed the 'most appropriate remembrance of the occasion'.

As the Wild West travelled north, two of the cowboys remained to challenge a pair of cyclists to a race, horse against machine, at the Agricultural Hall in Islington. The race was to take place over six days, eight hours per day using thirty horses, each mount changed every hour. The cowboys, Bronco Charlie Miller and Marv Beardsley, rode for a prize of £300 and although closely run, they won by two miles and two laps covering a total of 407 miles each.

The Wild West had moved on to Birmingham, opening for a short season at the Aston Lower Grounds where a covered stand was erected to contain 5000 people. The first performance was on 5th November 1887 and was given a tremendous reception by the crowds. Until 14th November, when electric carbon arc lighting was brought from London, only afternoon performances were possible, beginning at 3 p.m. Seats were bookable from Messrs. Rogers and Priestley's of Colmore Row at prices of 1, 2, and 3 shillings extra. The encampment was in the great hall, while the horses and other animals were stabled in the skating rink.

The Wild West moved on to Manchester, opening there on 17th December, 1887 at the racecourse, New Barnes, Salford, in a purpose built theatre next to the main stand, heated by steam, electrically lit and costing £15,000. The building, huge by standards of the day, was constructed of wood and brick by Messrs. Neills and Co., the whole enterprise being at the risk of businessmen R. Mansell and William Calder. The 8,000 seats were arranged like an amphitheatre, some forty feet from ground level, so that everyone would have a perfect view of the proceedings. The stage itself was rectangular, with one end extended into a semi-circle and the other curtained to form the backdrop behind which performers could assemble. There was also an iron curtain to comply with fire regulations. The Wild West building measured 600 feet long by 200 feet wide, and 80 feet high allowing a stage length of 140 feet. The rafters were painted bright red and white. Part of the stage was probably mobile, with scenery being constantly changed out of sight of the public to give a realism so far unknown to British audiences. The walls of the building were adorned with hunting trophies, banners and other western items to give atmosphere.

The Indian encampment was inside the main building, and to the rear of the structure a shed was erected to house the buffaloes, bear, deer and elks. At the other end, close to where the public entered, covered stalls were put up to sell refreshments and souvenirs.

*The custom-made building at Salford constructed for the Wild West.*

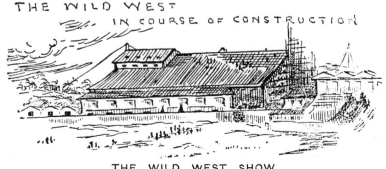

THE WILD WEST IN COURSE OF CONSTRUCTION

THE WILD WEST SHOW.

*A standard advertising block of a group of Indians in the encampment.*

Such a perfect venue allowed the finest performances given by the show in England. Split into seven distinct sections, some of the larger set-pieces were not even seen by London audiences. After the overture by the cowboy band, the programme began with orator Richmond, dressed in western garb, and carrying a rifle, entering forty feet from the ground on a simulated rocky outcrop. With his long side hair capped by a bald head, his magnificent voice reached all corners of the auditorium and after introducing the various groups in the initial revue, and of course Buffalo Bill, he remained to explain each aspect of the show.

The arena cleared for the first of the set-pieces, 'The Forest Primeval'. This showed America before the coming of the white man. Beginning at simulated dawn, a bear and a herd of deer were seen to cross a glade in a tangled forest, followed by buffalo pursued by Indian hunters with bows and arrows. After a tribal dance, the warriors were confronted by a band of hostiles and a battle ensued. The second act depicted the landing of the Pilgrim Fathers at Plymouth Rock with a sea backcloth and Indians showing some interest, and progressed to captain John Smith being saved by the Indian maiden, Pocahontas. As this scene closed, the next followed on immediately, showing the many aspects of Indian life on the frontier.

The backdrop changed again to give an impression of the rolling prairie stretching to the horizon. A drinking pool was visible to which the buffalo herd wandered, followed shortly by another bull which was hotly pursued by Buffalo Bill in a mock hunt. The scene developed with the appearance of an immigrant wagon train, drawn by oxen and mules. After camp was pitched around the water hole the pioneers were seen to fall asleep. It was here that the first of the major effects was used. A faint red light was discernible on the distant hills, growing in intensity and rolling across the stage until it seemed that the whole was engulfed in a raging prairie fire.

Indians, buffalo and other animals dashed through the camp to add to the confusion, a brilliant example of stage management and scenic display.

Feats of horsemanship and shooting followed including the riding of bucking horses by cowboys, followed by the 'Attack on a Settler's Cabin' in which Lillian Smith and Emma Hickok participated. Then came what Richmond described as 'The Reddest Page of Savage History', being loosely based around a military post on the frontier and Custer's demise. After a battle in which all soldiers were 'killed', the scene showed the battlefield by moonlight with fallen cavalrymen and standing horses. Buffalo Bill arrived to the rescue, 'too late', but returned a few minutes later to give an exhibition of shooting from the saddle.

The final act was perhaps the most complicated and the most exciting, opening with a view of a mining camp with the inhabitants going about their everyday life. This went on to show a shooting match, the capture of a horse thief, the arrival of the Pony Express and the Deadwood Stage. The coach was then attacked by Indians and saved by Buffalo Bill and the cavalry. It was here that huge Blackman air propellers turned the stage into a depiction of a cyclone, destroying the camp and tearing the cabins to pieces. Leaves and branches blew everywhere, adding to the effect. A fitting finale to what must have been a marvellous show.

Buffalo Bill was wined and dined by Manchester's businessmen and Freemasons who frequented the showgrounds like children in a toyshop. In response, Cody invited them to meals with the Wild West and organised horse races on the Salford track. So many local officials were invited to the first performance that many ordinary people had to stand to watch the show, but were allowed in free. The Mayor of Salford, Mr. Albert Dickens, wrote to Cody at Howard Street conveying good wishes for the show during its stay in the town.

One incident which detracted from the successes of the Wild West was the death of one of the Indians. The warrior was a Sioux named 'Surrounded', who died in the Hope Hospital from 'inflammation of the lungs'. He was twenty two years old and was interred in the Salford cemetery, the funeral attended by members of the Wild West, including the principal Sioux Chief, Red Shirt.

The last performance in Manchester was on April 30th 1888 at which the crowds refused to let Cody leave the arena, giving him an extended standing ovation. On Thursday 3rd May, almost as a farewell, a horserace was arranged between English thoroughbreds and American mustangs from the Wild West. This apparently was the second such race, although the date and outcome of the first is unrecorded. The race was a long affair with the Englishman, J. Latham, against Antonio Esquivel for the Americans, and many spectators arrived to view the contest.

Mounts were changed at each half mile post and the English horse at first showed the greater speed, gaining a short lead at the end of the first lap. This advantage was soon matched by the American rider's skill at changing mounts. Following a minor collision by the English horse, Esquivel took the lead by two furlongs. Latham began to make up lost ground steadily, but the race ended with the American winning by 400 yards. The race time was 22 minutes.

The day before, Wednesday the 2nd, some of the Wild West stock was auctioned. Lots were principally horses which brought only moderate interest and prices, although a matched pair of bay carriage horses received more attention and were sold to B. Goodall for £80. The auctioneer, Mr Edwin Bradshaw, then began his sale of other stock. Several well known circus owners were present, including George Sanger, who bought two elks for £40, two dappled mules at £21, and two American deer at £10. A buffalo sold to a Mr Cross of Liverpool, who also purchased four elks and a bear.

As Buffalo Bill departed by train from Manchester, the crowds watching sang 'Auld Lang Syne'. The Wild West was going home but it was to make one last performance in Hull before boarding the steamer, Persian Monarch. The first train of 18 wagons departed at ten o'clock with its cargo of buffalo, deer, horses and ponies. At eleven, the second train of 9 wagons left with Cody, the Indians, and other members of the company, and a last train followed with baggage and the Deadwood Stage coach. Transit arrangements were in the charge of Mr J. H. Williams, chief traffic inspector for the Hull and Barnsley Railway Company.

Cody arrived at Hull's Alexandra Dock at two-twenty. With him were Shybell, the assistant manager, Buck Taylor, Bronco Bill (Sioux interpreter) and Frank Richmond, the orator. On alighting from the train, Cody immediately boarded the Persian Monarch to inspect arrangements for the voyage home, where he was eventually joined by some of the ladies from the show, including his daughter Arta.

Standard advertising block used in advertisements.

host Bainton, he seemed to be equally 'un-understandable'."

What are we to make of such a statement? Presumably Buffalo Bill would have taken a drop or two with the captain of the Persian Monarch, and may have been slightly 'happy' to be going home. Is the 'Billingsgate tongue' a reference to bad language? Certainly the reporter would prefer to pen a column with some bite, but either way the outcome was the same. To the eternal embarrassment of the people of Hull, Buffalo Bill Cody, scout and showman, was trounced from their finest hotel. Buffalo Bill's comments are not recorded, but he probably made the best of that which the Imperial Hotel had to offer, and indeed if the reports are correct, also made the best of them the next evening, when a waiter was summoned by proprietor Bainton to escort him to bed. The same report suggests that Buffalo Bill had booked a room in three hotels in order that he would find one to his liking. The one at the Station Hotel from which he was cast out, one at the Imperial at which he eventually stayed, and one at the Manchester Hotel in George Street, owned by Mr Boniface Manchester.

If the reporter from the Arrow was to be believed, Cody did visit the Manchester for a few hours snooze before moving on. Even for such a flamboyant character as Buffalo Bill, such behaviour seems misrepresented and more likely rooms were booked for other members of the company, with the proprietor of the Manchester assuming the reservation was for Cody. It must be remembered that the article was published one week after the Wild West had departed for America, and Cody could therefore not reply. In 1888 the Hull Arrow, a small weekly magazine-type journal, had its offices in Bowlalley Lane. Its proprietors at this time were Abraham Johnson and Frederick William Guy.

Another article in the same issue deals with the show in a different way, if retaining something of the same irritating meandering. This reporter, who used the pseudonym ' the man with the carpet bag', although admiring the Indians in their stature, notes that ' their acquaintance with Pears soap and Springhead water appeared to be of a most limited character'. The full page article somewhat ramblingly wastes half of its

Shortly afterwards the little group proceeded to the Station Hotel, situated in the centre of the city by the Paragon passenger station, It was here that Buffalo Bill and a few others had planned to stay until leaving for America after the final performance. Other members of the staff were staying at the Queens and Manchester Hotels, while general performers and workers would be housed at the Alexandra Dock emigrant shed.

Upon presenting themselves at the Station Hotel, the proprietor, one Mr Jones, for some reason took a dislike to Cody's accent. Perhaps the following quote from the Hull Arrow (12th May 1888) explains more fully:-

"Again Bill of the Buffalo ilk certainly has not caused much delight in the bosoms of the hotelkeepers of this town. The good folks of 'the Station Hotel' in the first place, somehow or other, didn't exactly appear to appreciate his ability as a linguist - especially when he so fluently ejaculated in the Billingsgate tongue. They couldn't understand him at all, and he was consequently and subsequently informed that he must move. He did so and finally arrived at the 'Imperial', where to mine genial space on the charms of an Indian maiden of sixteen, and is sadly lacking in actual reportive value.

As the trains were unloaded on the Alexandra Dock that Thursday, some of the mounted cowboys formed a circle and herded the buffalo from their confinement. One report in a periodical named 'Morison's Amusements and Coming Events' with the title 'Hedon Road stampede' details how the buffalo broke away and headed through the dockyard onto the Hedon Road, past local public houses, pursued by mounted Sioux warriors and cowboys. Patrons of the pubs apparently stood at the doors, pint pots in hand with dropped jaws. Perhaps the scent of salt water promoted the bolting of the fifteen bison, which were eventually individually roped. Sadly this report is only second hand and despite considerable research, an original copy of this periodical containing the article has not been traced. But it is a wonderful story.

*Illustration from the programme.*

On the 5th of May, again in the Hull Arrow, a reporter detailing the entertainments offered at the theatres in the city's Carr Lane, mentions his seeing a telegram from Buffalo Bill in which the latter promised his patronage at one of these establishments. To whom the telegram was sent we are not informed, but Cody did indeed visit the theatre in Hull that Thursday evening, together with his daughter and other members of the Wild West. Unlike most other periodicals of the day, the Hull Arrow seemed to some extent to be either anti-American, or at least anti-Buffalo Bill, and seemed to take great delight in showing him in a poor light, both in word and in cartoon form. Unfortunately for researchers, this led to poor factual reporting, and little tangible detail.

While in Hull for these few days in May, 1888, the photographers Turner and Drinkwater managed to persuade Buffalo Bill, his daughter and other members of the cast, to sit for photographs. Turner and Drinkwater had an excellent reputation and the pictures were apparently of the finest quality, but sadly have eluded all efforts to find them. Perhaps they are lost forever or maybe lie waiting in a dusty attic for someone to discover them. The photographers originally had their studio at Elm Tree House, Anlaby, but Kelly's Directory of 1905 shows them removed to Regent House in the Anlaby district. Apart from photography, their expertise also extended into the fields of ivory miniatures and portrait painting. They eventually moved to London, and today no longer exist.

The single performance by the Wild West in Hull took part on the afternoon of Saturday, May 5th, 1888 at the old football ground, in the Mersey Street / Severn Street area of the city. While not the great extravaganza seen at Salford, it was to be the final chance for British audiences to see something of the show that had delighted Queen Victoria at Earle's Court. The Eastern Morning News, whose offices were at 42, Whitefriargate, Hull, had advertised the attraction from 28th April, although locals had known of the coming event for quite a considerable time before that. Other interesting adverts were also included, adjacent to that of the Wild West. One, possibly taken out by Cody and Co. stated:-

IMPORTANT NOTICE

WANTED 50 RULLIES,
To be on
THE HULL FOOTBALL GROUND
Holderness Road
TO-DAY (SATURDAY)
Before One o' Clock

3s. 6d will be paid at the ground for the use of each Rully for
the afternoon.
A rully was a flat cart drawn by horses. Beneath this was
another advert:-

BUFFALO BILL'S SHOW

WANTED, 50 LADS
To Sell Programmes

Apply at the FOOTBALL GROUND at 11
O' clock THIS MORNING

Beneath this was another small advert taken by Mr. Edward Boyd of the Hope Iron Works, Holderness Road, informing the public that he had had a private stand constructed to accommodate 400 people. It was brick built, giving a 'best view' with a 'grand elevation'. Potential patrons could contact him at the Iron Works, or at his private address given as 15, Durham St. Possibly Mr. Boyd was connected with the Football Club, for it is hard to see how such an enterprise would be otherwise allowed.

As there would only be one performance in Hull, the enclosed ground was a perfect choice, the two playing areas being made into one with the end stand moved to one side and temporary elevated stands erected. Also, the venue was fairly close to the Alexandra Dock, the street parade leaving that place at 2 o'clock and arriving at the showground just before 3 o'clock. A personal

friend of Buffalo Bill, one Mr. Twist of Salford, had been allowed to ride Cody's favourite horse, 'Charlie', and take part in the procession.

By late morning, spectators had started to make their way towards the Holderness Road, and between 12 o'clock and 3 o'clock most routes to the football ground were filled with continuous lines of wagonettes, tram cars and cabs, stretching as far back as Savile Street, in the city centre. Police arrangements were very good and constables had been stationed at intervals to keep traffic moving and to maintain a presence as pickpockets were known to ply their trade amongst pedestrians. Many people had taken advantage of special excursion trains organised by most of the local railway companies, bringing visitors from as far afield as West Yorkshire and the Midlands. The grandstands were also full of the 'fashionable set' of the city including the Mayor and other officials.

General admission was set at one shilling, with reserved stands two shillings and sixpence, and other stands were three shillings. The advertisements in the newspapers informed the public that, due to the large number of applications received for the reserved seats, the whole of one of the principal stands would be set apart for five shilling seats. Tickets could be obtained from Messrs. Gough & Davy of Savile Street (who exist to this day), and Mr. Holder of Whitefriargate.

The weather proved favourable and added to the holiday atmosphere, and the performance commenced promptly at 3 o'clock with a parade of the performers, entering from the west gate and introduced by the orator, Mr. Richmond. When the cast was drawn up before the grandstand, Buffalo Bill entered last of all to an overwhelming applause, mounted on a big grey horse and dressed in what the newspapers described as 'Mexican hunting garb'.

The performance continued with races between Mexicans, cowboys and Indians, a Pony Express sequence, followed by Johnny Baker's fine shooting and saddle-bronc riding. This latter section lasted about twenty minutes, and was followed by

Indians attacking the Deadwood coach.

Buffalo Bill at full gallop shooting at balls.

*Above and above right: Are pages from the souvenir book showing exciting scenes from the Wild West.*

more sharpshooting by Lillian Smith, the 'California Girl'. Annie Oakley had left the show in Birmingham to follow her own way for a while, so at that time Lillian was the only female star. She wore a blue velvet dress with gold trimmings and a broad brimmed western hat.

More races between female frontier riders followed, and then the attack on the Deadwood Stagecoach, 'successfully repulsed by scouts and cowboys, commanded by Buffalo Bill'. Another contest followed between Indian boys mounted on mustangs and Mexican thoroughbreds, and then Emma Hickok, stepdaughter of the famous Wild Bill gave an equestrian display with her high-school horses. The latter was very well received, gaining considerable applause.

*The back cover of the souvenir book which depicts the buffalo hunt.*

Next came 'Phases of Indian Life', including activities such as the setting up of camp and various dramatic dances. Cody then re-appeared to give a display of mounted marksmanship in which an Indian rider preceded him, throwing glass balls into the air, which when hit shattered in a shower of tinsel and wool streamers.

Perhaps the highlight of the show for the crowd was the simulated buffalo hunt in which the animals were herded around the ground, pursued by Buffalo Bill. On 18th April, 1887, at a meeting of the General Committee of the R.S.P.C.A., a report had been given by the secretary John Colam, with regard to his investigation into Buffalo Bill's Wild West. An inspection had been carried out following complaints by Lady McKenna. What these complaints were and the recommendations of the R.S.P.C.A. are not recorded but it is likely that they were unfounded for two reasons. Firstly, at a time when animal rights were virtually unrecognised by the general public, Cody was on several occasions reported by the newspapers in a way that emphasised his kindness and consideration to his stock. Secondly, there were many rivals such as George Sanger, who would have made much of bad publicity for the Wild West. Also, the livestock was valuable and as much a part of the show as the humans, so it would therefore be common sense to ensure good treatment of the animals.

The final act that Saturday afternoon was the attack by hostile Indians upon a lone scout, the latter being saved in the nick of time by Buffalo Bill. This brought the show to a close, lasting a little over one hour, and as the crowds left, the cowboy band played 'God Save the Queen'.

As the Wild West had unfolded before the official audience, others looked on from a distance. The Hull Critic, another small magazine published at the time, reported (in an article entitled 'Wesleyan Ways and Cody's Cowboys'), that the Brunswick Wesleyan Sunday School and Chapel situated next to the football ground had let their windows to onlookers for one shilling per head. The Critic's opinion was that Wesleyanism was rigid in its religious views (and also illogical and inconsistent), and while it was deserving of credit for ingenuity, suggested that the money be handed over to the Hull Royal Infirmary lest discredit be brought on the Wesleyan faith. True to its name, the Critic also reported that although the show was thoroughly enjoyed by the crowds, there was a lack of 'blood and thunder and kill-all expressions' on the part of the performers.

ALEXANDRA DOCK, HULL.

Buffalo Bill and the cast rode back to the Alexandra Dock through the Hull streets, which were lined with people eager for a last look at the Wild West. Messrs. Wilson & Co., the shipping agents, had made arrangements for the swift embarkation of the animals and passengers alike with all necessary dispositions for a prompt departure when the tide allowed. One of the dock foremen, Edward E. Smalley, was present at the loading and

*The Alexandra Dock, Hull from where the Wild West sailed for home in 1888..*

apparently cheekily asked Buffalo Bill for a hat, which was duly given as a parting gift. The hat, unfortunately now lost, was handed down to his grandson, R. W. Smalley, who thereafter had trouble convincing school friends that it was the genuine article.

55

*An illustration from an original envelope showing Mexican Joe (Colonel Joe Shelley), with whose show Black Elk eventually enjoined.*

Meanwhile, when all were settled aboard the Persian Monarch, a luncheon was provided for Buffalo Bill, his staff, and also those of Wilson & Co. that were present. On the dockside, a considerable number of spectators stayed until around 7 o' clock, at which time they began to disperse. Up to then a friendly interchange of conversation took place between onlookers and show people, with many on the quayside asking if Buffalo Bill might make a last appearance. Alas they were disappointed. At 3 o' clock, as dawn was breaking and watched only by a very few, the Persian Monarch was released from her berth and edged out into the Humber, bound for New York. Apart from humans, horses and the buffalo aboard ship, there were elks, mules, donkeys, a parrot, a crow and a monkey. Hundreds of Hullensians made their way down to the dock during Sunday afternoon, hoping to see the departure, but the Wild West had gone.

The company which left Hull however, was incomplete. Four of the Indians, for whatever reason, had failed to answer roll call and sail home with the show. Two were never heard from again.

One Indian, Black Elk, eventually made his way to France after joining Mexican Joe's wild west show. In France he lived with a French woman and when Cody returned to Europe two years later, Black Elk found the show. A joyful reunion followed and Cody gave the Indian the choice of returning home or staying with the Wild West. The Sioux decided to return home. Cody paid his passage and gave him ninety dollars. Later, Black Elk wrote a book (Black Elk Speaks) describing his adventures. It is an interesting if somewhat strange publication, but relates to Buffalo Bill in an excellent light.

One of the cowboys, by the name of Taylor, had decided to stay to visit relatives in England. He had immigrated to America from Hull, and across the Atlantic had eventually joined Cody's show. His father, then deceased, had been the town auctioneer and proprietor of the Admiral Hawk public house, in Hessle, near Hull. His brother, another publican, kept the Oxford in North Street. Taylor planned to rejoin the Wild West after his visit, via a Liverpool Liner.

The Hull News on 12th May, 1888, gave some interesting views on the Indians aboard ship. The reporter, who with others was permitted to accompany the Wild West aboard the Persian Monarch until the vessel reached the channel, found them of a much quieter disposition than the 'rollicking cowboys', and unlike the latter showed little interest in 'firewater'. Some surprise was also shown when it was discovered that the Indians seemed to prefer to share a cigarette, rather than the peace pipe.

They were to be found on deck in blanket clad groups at all hours of the day or night. Their ability to consume great quantities of beef (about two pounds per person per meal) amazed the reporters, and also the effortless speed at which it was eaten.

At 6 o' clock, after steaming steadily down the Humber, course was set off the Newsand. Many of the reporters remained on deck all night and as the sea was smooth, some decided to get a little sleep before breakfast. The weather that Sunday was perfect and enjoyed by all, especially by some of the cowboys who played poker. The Indians were also fond of playing cards and were said to have perfect 'poker faces'. As the Persian Monarch steamed south, Cody and others of his staff relaxed on the promenade deck, on lounging chairs covered with buffalo robes, and indulged in reading or conversation.

That night, around 11 o' clock, the steamer encountered a fog bank and Captain Bristow ordered the engines to be slowed, progressing by means of the lead. At regular intervals, the steam whistle was sounded keeping everyone awake, until at 1 o' clock on Monday morning, anchor was dropped off Dover in order for the North Sea Pilot to be landed. Hicks, the pilot, was obliged to take charge of the Santiago, which was expected at Gravesend that day. Captain Bristow ordered two lifeboats to be swung out in case there might be need to render assistance to other vessels in the fog, or indeed to his own passengers and crew.

As day dawned, the fog remained dense for a while, but when it eventually cleared, Bristow ordered the anchor to be weighed and the ship proceeded slowly ahead. Again the steam whistle was continually blown but without hearing a return reply from other vessels. The fog thickened again and once more the Persian Monarch was forced to stop. Two hours later, it cleared again, and Dungeness was seen off the starboard beam. As the sun rose the captain ordered full steam ahead, but yet again by noon the fog was thicker than ever and the ship stopped once more. Forward lookouts were doubled, and a hand bell sounded at the stern for the next three hours until quite suddenly, the fog finally cleared and brilliant sunlight took its place.

*A contemporary press cartoon using the Wild West's visit to illustrate problems within the Government.*

The temperature rose considerably and overcoats were cast away. Approaching the Isle of Wight, another vessel hove into view. It was the Wilson liner, Santiago, and as she passed, the usual nautical courtesies were exchanged. Ventnor was passed, then the

Needles, and a course was set for the Portland breakwater. It was a pleasant evening and while the cowboy band entertained the ship's company with British, American and Scottish tunes, some of those inclined took to dancing. Later, Buffalo Bill remained up until quite late in his stateroom, entertaining the pressmen, who were making the most of every second with him.

By eleven thirty, the breakwater was reached and the anchor dropped. Captain Bristow had consulted with Cody regarding the amount of meat in storage aboard the ship. Cody was happy with the amount, providing that a normal passage was anticipated, and that there was an excess margin of 1000lbs, besides live chickens and sheep. Bristow, however, decided to lay in a further 500lbs of beef and a further six sheep, to be obtained at Portland.

While in Hull, the Persian Monarch had undergone some mechanical refits, and before crossing the Atlantic, Bristow had decided to take a few hours at Portland for adjustments. Those accompanying the Wild West were due to disembark that night, but the minor sea trials allowed them a little longer on board. The Hull News correspondent was invited to visit the stabling arrangements with Buffalo Bill, and noted the recognition showed by many of the horses when Cody approached them. Some animals were penned on the main deck but some were at a lower level due to the ship's excellent ventilation. Cody remarked upon the superior arrangements of the Persian Monarch compared with the State of Nebraska, the vessel which brought the show over from America. The main hatches were able to be kept open for much of the time due to a three foot high combing which would have kept out quite high seas. Even if the covers were closed, up-cast and down-cast ventilation systems were installed and would have kept the animal stalls cool.

Accommodation for the humans was on the lower deck, but apparently the ship proved very comfortable, the only noted setback being the distance from the galley to the dining room, which also served as a lounge. The Deadwood Stagecoach was lashed on the upper deck, and many feared for its survival should bad weather be encountered, as it was even then seen to be in a poor state of repair.

While the reporters waited on deck for departure, they noticed four young men already seated in the boat which had returned with the fresh meat. Looking very gloomy indeed, they were stowaways who had been found after continual routine searches of the ship. They were fairly, if firmly treated by the captain and crew. Whatever his personal views, Bristow would certainly have known that if stowaways were caught by the American authorities, he would have been fined, the miscreants imprisoned to await the return journey, and the captain charged for their upkeep. Suspicions that stowaways might be on board had been very strong since before leaving Hull. Due to the nature of the passengers, and their free run of the ship, it would have been easy for someone to sneak aboard and hide in the stock pens, or other parts of the vessel. All hatchways had been left open to provide as much ventilation as possible for the animals. Before leaving the Alexandra Dock, the captain had ordered all of Cody's people to muster and a roll called while the crew searched the ship. The list proved correct and no one at that time was found, and it was Monday evening before the searches proved successful.

The boat conveyed the stowaways ashore and when the reporters followed three hours later, nothing further was seen of them. Most of the newsmen had slept in their clothing, not knowing what time they would be landed, and Cody did the same, in order to be there to bid them 'goodbye'.

It was cold and grey when the time came to bid farewell and as the Englishmen wished Buffalo Bill and the Wild West a good crossing, the latter assured them of a warm welcome should they ever visit America.

As the gentlemen of the press were rowed ashore they saw the huge 'Ironclad', Hercules, getting up steam to leave the breakwater in order to take part in gun practice. Also moored nearby was the old training ship Boscawen, a veteran of the siege of Sebastopol during the Crimean War. This was her last active service. According to Mr. Cox, Wilson's agent, the Boscawen had been taken to Portsmouth a few months earlier to be docked prior to being broken up, but her planking and general state proved to be as sound as the day she was built, and so was reprieved as a training vessel.

Refreshments were taken by the reporters at the Breakwater Hotel, after which several took a stroll in the direction of the Portland Prison, and observed convicts being lined out in squads, in preparation for work in the quarries. Elsewhere, prison guards were engaged in firing practice under the watchtowers of the prison. If a prisoner escaped, a black flag was hoisted and a gun fired. This had happened a short time previously but the man was recaptured with four stolen sovereigns.

And so the Persian Monarch steamed out of British waters carrying Cody and the Wild West home. Despite the triumphs of the visit, one last unfortunate incident occurred to mar the successes. 'Charlie', Buffalo Bill's old war-horse had walked his last parade in Hull. Cody had spent a considerable amount of time with him in his stall below decks, and on the morning of 14th May, took him some sugar. An hour later, a groom informed Cody that the horse was unwell. The scout stayed with him for much of the next two days, but suffering from possible lung problems, the animal's condition rapidly worsened. He died at 2 o' clock on the morning of 17 May.

Charlie lay in state on deck that day, covered in a canvas shroud, and the 'Stars and Stripes'. The horse was a half-blood Kentucky stallion and Cody, much distressed, gave a funeral oration before the ship's company at eight in the evening. Charlie was to be buried at sea. It had been Cody's intention to take the horse home and bury him on American soil, but due to health hazards, this was decided against. As Charlie slid beneath the waves, the cowboy band played 'Auld Lang Syne', and the ship's cannon was fired in salute.

The old horse had been a favourite, ridden by everyone, great and small, from children to Grand Duke Michael of Russia. Although it cannot be confirmed, Charlie, who was twenty when he died, may have been the horse that Cody was riding during his famous 'duel' with Yellow Hand.

The Wild West was enthusiastically welcomed home when the Persian Monarch reached New York. It was seen by many as an event of national importance. As the cowboy band played 'Yankee Doodle' the Persian Monarch left quarantine and berthed at Bechtel's Wharf on Staten Island on 20th May. Recent improvements meant it was the first time that an ocean going steamer of her size, draught and class had done so. This was an event of real commercial importance to the port of New York, demonstrating the marine value of ten more miles of coastline.

Steamers and tugs converged, conveying many prominent citizens out to escort the vessel to her berth. The first foreign visit of the Wild West was over, but it would not be the last.

# WHEELS, WAGONS, WATER AND WINGS. . .

*Transporting the Wild West over land and sea. Trains, ships, wagons, and an 'impostor' in the air. . .*

## TRAINS. . . (1888)

When the Wild West first came over to England in 1887, to take part in Queen Victoria's Jubilee celebrations, it was not seen as the great travelling show that it had been in America, or indeed as it would be seen in later visits. The British public saw the show at extensive engagements in only three towns, London, Birmingham and Manchester. Then, leaving Manchester to return home in May 1888, the show travelled cross country to Hull, giving one final afternoon performance in that city before boarding ship for the passage back to America.

Although little information survives, regarding the actual detail of the trains used during the first visit of the show, something can be gleaned from the newspapers and magazines of the period. Not at this stage having the benefit of their own rolling stock, the Wild West would have had to deal with local Railway companies.

About 7 o' clock on the evening of 3rd May 1888, a train carrying much of the Wild West's baggage steamed into Hull's Alexandra Dock. Aboard were many non-live properties including the Deadwood Stagecoach. On the afternoon of Friday 4th May, another train arrived just before 2 o' clock, carrying the buffalo, elk, mustangs and bucking horses. Many gathered to watch the arrival of the show and the de-training. Earlier, at Manchester's Victoria Station, Mr. Sedgewick, of the Lancashire & Yorkshire Railway Company, was given the responsibility for transit arrangements, jointly with Mr. J.H. Williams of the Hull & Barnsley Railway. The Hull & Barnsley (Hull, Barnsley and West Riding Junction Railway and Dock Company), at this time formed the main line of communication between Hull and the South and West Yorkshire coalfields. It had junctions with the Lancashire & Yorkshire railway (at Hensall), the Great Northern Railway, the Midland Railway and the Great Central Railway.

It was Hull & Barnsley rolling stock which carried the Wild West into Hull. The Alexandra Dock at this time was being utilised to a great extent for timber traffic, but passenger vessels were not uncommon. Around 1885, ninety five per cent of emigrant traffic from Eastern Europe, bound for America, was handled at the dock by the Hull & Barnsley. Plans were approved on June 1885, for short term accommodation of emigrants in the north west corner, close to the dock signal box. The emigrant ships usually docked in Hull on Fridays or Saturdays, in time for special trains carrying transit passengers on to Liverpool the following Monday. Escaping from Czarist Russia, many of the emigrants preferred to camp in Hull's Pearson Park, rather than be enclosed by the walls of the dock accommodation. For this reason, the Monday trains were eventually started from the Cannon Street halt.

The Wild West flyer (printed black on blue paper), posted in May 1888 to advertise the coming of the show, states 'Excursions on all Railways', showing the willingness of the railway companies to inter-schedule to take advantage of this one-off event.

Little is known of the type of locomotives actually used to pull the Wild West trains in England, but excursion traffic for the Hull Fair a few years later saw the introduction of Lancashire & Yorkshire and Midland 0-6-0's and 4-4-0's on the Hull & Barnsley line.

## TRAINS. . .(1891)

Returning to English shores from Belgium in 1891, as part of its European tour, the Wild West docked at the port of Grimsby in Lincolnshire. Here, arrangements had been made with the Manchester, Sheffield and Lincolnshire Railway to convey the show to its first engagement in Leeds. Another chapter deals with the help given to the Wild West by a deputation of directors of the MS & L in its quarantine problems in 1891. Eventually 47 of the company's trucks, in the form of flat and stock cars in three sections, moved everything to Leeds, lock, stock and stagecoach.

*Left: Newspaper Advertisement.*

Another indication of the relationship of the railways to potential patrons of the Wild West can be seen in the following verse, taken from 'The Yorkshireman', another of the small magazine periodicals, dated July 1st 1891 :-

"To the Wild West-Aye-to the West," as Henry Russell used to sing.
I've always thought must be a most exhilarating thing;
And when I found that I could reach that land he called so free.
For quite an inexpensive sum _ I said, "There I will be";
I vowed I'd take the warpath - in a Midland railway train -
To see how Injuns capture scalps upon the prairie plain.

So in a first-class carriage you had found the dogg'rel bard,
A smoking of his calumet along with his good 'pard;
Bound for the West, the "Wild, Wild West", as seen at Cardigan,

So stepping off at Armley on the train he quickly ran;
He hurried from the station with a war whoop weird and wild,
Through the primeval forests, there to seek the prairie child."

Strange prose by today's standards. For those unfamiliar with the area, 'Cardigan' refers to the area of Leeds (Cardigan Fields) where the show took place, with Armley being the station at which the visitor to the Wild West would disembark.

## TRAINS. . . (1903/4)

The last tour of the UK by the Wild West is the one for which most information remains, regarding the railway connections, but we must first go back seven years.

The 1894 season at Brooklyn, New York, had been disappointing, and Cody as usual needed money. Nate Salsbury was ill and would never again take a truly active part in the management of the show. Salvation came in the shape of James A. Bailey, a partner of the late Barnum, who had died in 1891. Bailey agreed to take a share of the Wild West's profits in exchange for providing transportation for the show and local expenses. When it was decided that the show return to Europe, transport was ready and waiting in England in the form of a purpose-built show train.

To explain fully, we must follow the affairs of another great show. Barnum & Bailey's three ring circus, the 'Greatest Show on Earth', had been brought over in November 1897 to tour the UK and Europe from 1898. As in America, only railways could transport such a huge show at the speed necessary to maintain its itinerary of one-day stands. In America, purpose-built rolling stock had been constructed in the form of elephant cars, stock cars, flat cars, passenger cars and an advance booking car(s). Because of the restricted loading gauge in Europe it was pointless shipping these vehicles across the Atlantic, and therefore new rolling stock was needed.

While in London in 1896, Bailey had met W.R. Renshaw, whose heavy engineering company was based at Stoke on Trent. Renshaws were experienced in the manufacture of railway vehicles for foreign companies and after meeting Bailey again in America, Renshaw returned with a contract to build specialised circus cars. An extra car was eventually needed to replace the pony car, which was wrecked in an accident in Germany in 1901. The total number of cars constructed is a little uncertain but the breakdown was probably:-

35 Flat Cars Numbers 125 - 159
16 Stock Cars Numbers 107 - 122
1 Pony Car Number 106
3 Elephant Cars Numbers 103 - 105
1 Camel Car Number 102
1 Trunk Car Number 100 (Baggage)
1 Led Stock Car Number 101 (Llamas etc.)
8 Sleeping Cars Numbers 50-57
1 Private Car (James Bailey / Buffalo Bill)
1 Advertising Car Number 1

Records do not clearly show if the private car was additional or part of the original eight sleepers. The Locomotive magazine of 1897 quotes nine sleepers.

Renshaw's Phoenix Works was situated alongside the North Staffordshire Railway, between Stoke and Etruria, and the circus vehicles were built in 1897-8, in time for the tour. Just over half of the rolling stock had been built by March 1898 and after trial runs on the NSR, was handed over to Barnum & Bailey, the last of the cars, including Bailey's private carriage, delivered in Glasgow. The complete show train was used for the journey from Glasgow to Edinburgh on the night of 16th/17th July 1898. To accommodate regulations laid down by the London County Council when the circus opened there on 27th December 1897, Renshaws also built a safety fire curtain of steel and asbestos in record time and at a cost of £50,000.

Because the construction of the cars was to be of American design, an engineer from Barney & Smith of Dayton, Ohio (who had built the American rolling stock), had been brought over to England to supervise operations. Many of the circus road vehicles and wagons were extremely large. To accommodate these and bring the cars within the British loading gauge, the American designs had to be reduced in both height and width. All of the vehicles were 54 feet long and were carried on two four-wheel bogies. Due to their long bodies, the cars were only eight feet wide to allow for the 'throw over' on sharp curves, where there might be a platform on the inside. On some cars, clearance to rail level was only seven and a half inches.

All vehicles were fitted with both vacuum and Westinghouse air brakes, to comply with the preferences of the various railway companies in whose areas they would be travelling. At this time the majority of companies used vacuum brakes. American Janney buckeye automatic couplers were used because British couplings could not be fitted to the flatcars and sleeping cars at the correct height. These automatic couplers also speeded up the operation of reforming the trains. The centres of the couplers were only 30" above rail level, 4.5" lower than the American standard and 11" lower than that for British type couplings. On occasion, however, adapter rods were available to connect British and American couplings. Eight stock cars (100-109) were connected, at one end only, with the buckeyes, while the other end carried normal spring buffers and screw couplers.

These vehicles were used as end cars. The circus vehicles were formed into four trains, two of sixteen and two of seventeen cars with one of the dual couplers at each end. A third class brake carriage was connected at the rear of each train, and these were the equivalent of American cabooses.

When the Wild West took over the trains, the four sections were reduced to just three, comprising some fifty cars. During this time, the vehicles remained the property of Barnum & Bailey, and circus personnel were included within the Wild West company to carry out loading and unloading duties, under the supervision of their Assistant Master of Transportation. For some reason, which is unclear, brake cars were fitted to the heads of two sections of the Wild West trains but not the third, bringing the total number of vehicles to fifty-five.

Flat Cars (125 - 159)
One major problem was with the 35 flat cars. Two types were constructed, one with vacuum and air brakes, and one with 'through' piping and usually operated in pairs, one of each type. The two types were of a different structure, the through piped version having heavy underframe bracing. Decking consisted of planks with an outer plank at right angles, running along the edge of the car. Sometimes, platforms would not be available, and so they were designed for loading from ground level by means of portable ramps. End ramps could be used with the rakes of flat cars. The decks were built 11" below normal British standard, and consequently, seven foot long bogies were used with smaller diameter wheels. Finding the 28", all-steel, disc

*This photograph, although of Barnum & Bailey 'Greatest Show on Earth', will give an idea of how the trains were unloaded. Note the end ramp just visible at the lower left.*

wheels unavailable in the UK, it was necessary to obtain them from the famous Krupps company, of Essen in Germany. Some of the flat cars were originally fitted with American style handbrakes on a removable stanchion but were not considered essential, and were probably removed prior to service as they obstructed loading activities. The flat cars were authorised by the Railway Clearing House to carry a load of 60,000lbs., or twenty-six and three-quarter tons.

Stock Cars (107 - 122)
In all, sixteen stock cars were made, having a similar underframe to the flat cars. Again, built to American design, these vehicles also had heavy horizontal planking fixed to an external frame, with clearance allowances made for ventilation and cleaning-out. In the centre of each side, was a pair of outward opening swing doors, secured with a drop in bar, and at each end was a small sliding door for further ventilation and access. Windows in

*Flat car wearing Barnum & Bailey livery later used by the Wild West.*

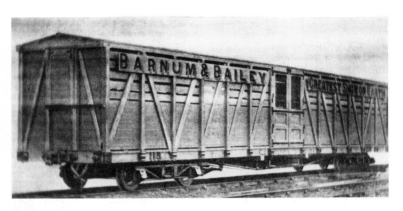

*Stock car in B & B livery.*

the slide doors were unglazed but had heavy, vertical, metal bars. Several of the stock cars were of a slightly different design to allow for their various original functions, i.e. camel car, etc. Five of the stock cars were dual fitted with British and American draw-gear to act as the end vehicles as already mentioned, the coupling equipment fitted at a considerable height above the underframe. To facilitate loading and unloading, a wooden ramp was carried on brackets which were attached to truss rods below the doors.

*Sleeping car, originally built for the B & B circus and later used by Buffalo Bill's Wild West.*

BOGIE SLEEPING CAR, 54 ft. long.
One of 68 specially built for Inter-European Traffic.

Pony Car (101) and Lead Stock Car (102)
These vehicles were similar to the elephant cars but with shallow, peaked roofs, like the standard British stock cars, and were designed to be end cars. The Pony car was the only one of its kind , having a double deck, the upper being accessed by an internal ramp. Inside, at one end, there was sleeping accommodation for the grooms. They were built with vertical boarding around an internal frame with a pair of large, central doors. A smaller door was built into the framework between the main doors and the end of the car.

The elephant cars (103 - 105) were not used by Buffalo Bill and therefore, for the purpose of this book, are not applicable. These cars remained at the winter quarters at Cliffe Vale, Stoke-on-Trent, along with other unused rolling stock. Cliffe Vale, adjacent to Renshaw's Phoenix Works, had also been the circus HQ and winter quarters. Built and leased to the circus (and Buffalo Bill) by W.R. Renshaw & Co., the site was situated on the west side of the North Staffordshire Railway, between Stoke and Etruria.

Passenger Cars (50 - 57)
The eight passenger cars were built to accommodate the staff and performers of 'The Greatest Show on Earth', and ultimately the cowboys, Indians and other performers of Buffalo Bill's Wild West. The private car, used by Bailey and Buffalo Bill, may have been a ninth vehicle, and not a part of the original eight, being converted with a little more comfort in mind. This carriage had an office, a bedroom and 'living room' accommodation. Buffalo Bill's private car in America was 'No. 50' and had been originally named 'Mayflower' and built for the opera singer Adelina Patti. Bought from the Pennsylvania Railroad, it was renamed 'Cody' and had four staterooms, living quarters, dining room and kitchen.

The Renshaw built passenger coaches, more than the other part of the trains, must have stood out considerably to British viewers, being very much different to standard carriages of the period. The cars had vertical boarding on an internal frame with extended roofing covering end verandas. Window arrangements varied a little on some carriages. While some had seventeen per side, others (standard) had sixteen with a blank. The substantial underframes had heavy timber cross members with cast iron queen posts, and adjustable truss rods ran outside the inner ends of the bogies. There was a door at each end of the carriage leading onto the veranda, and opposite this, a wrought iron handrail. Like the freight vehicles, the passenger cars had 28" steel disc wheels to accommodate the reduction in height, and all were fitted with buckeye couplers and were without buffers. There were some slight differences in the construction of the passenger cars, some having larger verandas and others with different window plans. An oval plate carried on the headstock was inscribed:-

'J. A. Bailey - Owner - Stoke-on-Trent'

Sleeping arrangements were certainly of a 'no frills' type for standard workers, with slatted wooden bunks, four-high on each side of a narrow walkway, allowing some seventy persons to be accommodated per coach. No cooking facilities were fitted and the only apparent concession to 'comfort' was the inclusion of a toilet at each end of the car. It has to be remembered that the time spent by staff aboard the coaches was probably minimal and spent asleep after a day's hard work. A Sleeping Car Attendant supervised the cars, with a porter in each one. The performers were required to pay the porter a small sum per week for minor services such as shoe cleaning etc.

Advance Advertising Car (Number One)
The operation of this most interesting vehicle is dealt with in another section of this book. With a staff of twenty, it travelled up to three weeks ahead of the show by scheduled services and was responsible for confirming sites, billposting and general advance advertising. Unlike other vehicles built by Renshaws, this car did not have 28" wheels. Instead it ran at standard height on 3 foot diameter wheels. Again it was fitted with Westinghouse and vacuum brakes, and also with British buffers and couplings. Perhaps more than the other vehicles, the 'Advance' looked typically American in design with clerestory roof and end verandas, the latter having a high step up due to the restrictive loading gauge.

It was built with vertical boarding on an internal frame, each side of the vehicle having a large sliding door at one end but differing window arrangements. A single window near the door was balanced at the opposite end by a cluster of three more. A large central box was secured underneath the car to accommodate equipment, while the inside was fitted with an office, sleeping accommodation, workspace, benches and cupboards.

Livery
For use by both the circus and the Wild West, Number One was painted white with underframe probably dark green and wheel trim in white also. Lettering would have been in various combinations of patriotic red and blue, but sometimes in gold with blue shading. Shields, red with gold highlights and lettering, were painted at intervals around the vehicle containing various inspiring slogans. In circus service the car carried twelve shields and for the Wild West six, the area covered by lettering instead.

Passenger cars were originally painted bright lake (maroon) with gold lettering, and presumably lined in an appropriate colour which is unknown. The underframes and wheels were dark green and lined in yellow. Later, when the circus was in Europe and travelling the German State Rys, colours may have changed, for the Locomotive Magazine reporting the progress of the trains, states that the cars were bright red with dark lake around the mouldings.

Stock cars and flat cars were in Barnum & Bailey traditional yellow livery and appropriately lettered. Underframes and ironwork were black. Some reports, when the rolling stock was in use by Buffalo Bill, state that the colour of these vehicles was still yellow. Others, possibly more accurate, state that they were orange, and it is more likely that this was the case.

Organising the Trains
The trains used by Buffalo Bill's Wild West in the UK between 1902 and 1904 were organised in the following three sections:-

Train Number Three :-

Engine & 3rd Class Brake Car

1 Stock Car
7 Flat Cars
5 Sleeping Cars
1 Stock car
1 3rd Class Brake Car

Length 756 feet
Weight 351 tons

Train Number One :-

Engine

1 Stock Car
7 Flat cars
5 Stock Cars
3 Sleeping Cars
1 Box Sleeper (Pony Car)
1 Stock Car
1 3rd Class Brake Car

Length 972 feet
Weight 432 tons

Plus Advertising Car (Number One)

Train Number Two :-

Engine & 3rd Class Brake Car

1 Stock Car (Camel Car)
15 Flat Cars
1 Truck Car (Baggage)
1 3rd Class Brake Car

Length 918 feet
Weight 421 tons

Total lengths including engine and two brake carriages:-

Train number Three :- 306 yards

Train number one :- 378 yards

Train number two :- 360 yards

In September 1904, one flat car was withdrawn from no. 2 train and the lead stock car, which was previously unused by the Wild West and no longer and end car, was transferred to train no. 1.

The trains were restricted to a maximum speed of 25 m.p.h., and apart from Barnum & Bailey operatives travelling with the Wild West there would also be other railway officials and guards on board. Rates for the movement of such show trains was sixpence per mile and a halfpenny per passenger, charged by the shortest route. A terminal charge was also imposed at both ends of the journey and these charges would cover shunting costs. Carriage rates for the show would have been agreed with the railway companies via the Railway Clearing House.

An article in the 'World's Fair' paper of March 1951 refers to the workings of Buffalo Bill's trains in 1903 on the Great Western, over the Bushbury Exchange Branch between Bushbury No. 1 and Cannock Road Junction Box. Reference was from an original railway movement sheet for the period and states that they were. .

"in accordance with the instructions laid down for the working of the Royal Train."

There are also references to members of the Wild West possessing bicycles, which when carried on the railways, were charged for in the normal manner.

Loading and unloading for both Buffalo Bill and Barnum & Bailey was no mean feat. The equipment and stock packed last was that which would be unloaded first, being needed to rebuild the show site from scratch at the next venue. Outside, as the show performed its last act, everything not needed was being dismantled, ready for moving on. Everything had its place and was stored in exactly the same position, year after year, to ensure the smooth running of the show. Immediately upon reaching the next town, the goods yards would buzz with a flurry of activity. Every man and horse knew their places and jobs to the letter. Sometimes, the showground was some way from the rail depot and so a day's work could be long and hard for the teamsters, when several return trips were needed.

*Another view of the uloading of a B & B circus train showing the end ramps and horses waiting to take up the wagons.*

Returning to the train after the performances, the draught horses were released and the wagons taken by 'pull-up' teams which would then drag them up steel ramps at the end of the rake of flat cars, guided by an operative known as the 'run-poler'. Once the wagons were up, the team was again replaced by a two horse hitch known as the 'hook team', with the draught animals pulling the road vehicles the length of the train from ground level, over connecting plates between the cars. Responsible for this activity was the 'deck-poler'. This job was particularly hazardous and a man could risk injury being knocked from the train, or from moving wagons in the restricted work space. A Master of Transportation, who travelled with train no. 2, oversaw the operation, usually with an assistant, along with eleven train-men and four teamsters to load the whole show onto the trains.

## LOCOMOTIVES
Although little hard information has come to light regarding the engines used by the Wild West, some deductions can be made. Locomotives would vary as the show was moved over from one railway company to another. For example, the 'Barnum' class 2-4-0's would certainly have been used as it passed through on the Great Western Railway.

Built in 1889, the 'Barnums', or 3206 class engines, gained their nickname entirely due to the fact that they had been used to haul the circus trains on the GWR. The class consisted of twenty locomotives numbered 3206 - 3225 (Swindon Works Nos. 1137 - 1156). Reverting to previous GWR design, having outside sandwich frames, they were probably the last of their type built in the world. Allen-Richardson balanced side valves were fitted beneath the cylinders, the boilers being traditional Swindon design with two rings, brass covered dome and flush firebox. The 'Barnums' worked through into the Twentieth Century, the last two withdrawn from the Wellington Shed, Crewe, 3210 on 4th March, and 3222 on 5th March, 1937. All except one of these locomotives (3218) ran over one million miles in their lifetimes. Engines used to haul the heavy show trains would have to be substantial, and would need to have vacuum or Westinghouse brake equipment fitted. While the show was travelling between stands in Scotland, on the Great North of Scotland Railway, trains were double-headed, two locomotives needed to negotiate severe gradients. Later, when travelling from Stranraer to Dumfries, the big 0-8-0 steam engines of the Caledonian Railway Company were used. These powerful locos were introduced in 1901, and were the first eight coupled engines employed in Scotland to haul heavy trains of 30 ton, steel bogie wagons in the Lanarkshire coalfield. Some of these wagons were also manufactured by W. R. Renshaw & Co., and also fitted with Westinghouse brakes.

During this part of Buffalo Bill's tour of Scotland, an incident took place when the show train was approaching a viaduct under repair on the way to Loch Skerrow. Following a wrong warning light shown by a watchman, the train was stopped on the viaduct on a 1 in 76 incline. Losing momentum, the heavy train was unable to gain purchase on the rails even after sanding, and it was decided to split it into two sections.

Railwaymen on the scene were unfamiliar with the American couplings and were unable to proceed until the Barnum & Bailey train men showed them how. The first part of the train was taken on to Loch Skerrow and the engine then returned with the 3rd class brake car to recover the second section.

Buffalo Bill's tour of the European mainland ended at Ghent in Belgium on 21st September 1906. Cody and the show returned to America and the rolling stock was returned to England, to be purchased as one lot by E. E. Cornforth, a used stock dealer of Trentham, Stoke. Between 1908 and 1910, they were sold on again, the Alexandra (Newport) Docks and Railway of South Wales purchasing 23 flat cars, 2 elephant cars and 3 passenger cars. At this time, Renshaws reworked two of the flat cars and fitted British drawgear in order to move the whole section, in one train, to South Wales. The passenger coaches were also modified by Renshaws at a cost of £51.10s per car, and were eventually used as railmotor trailers between Pontypridd and Caerphilly. These passenger coaches eventually came into the ownership of the Great Western Railway, one used from 1920 as a stationary office for the mechanical foreman at the Newport Pill shed. This carriage was grounded in 1923 but probably survived until 1963. The others were withdrawn from service in 1926. In 1927, one of the coaches was stored at Foss Cross on the old Midland and South Western Junction line, apparently condemned. The other was also subsequently grounded, where it remained until 1970.

Although the final fate of much of the rolling stock is unknown, we know that some of the stock cars were purchased by the Chatterley-Whitfield Colliery. They were used to convey miners to work, from Burslem to the pit-head, and because of their history, became known as 'monkey vans'. The private car used by Buffalo Bill and Bailey was also reworked by Renshaws, according to instructions from Cornforth, being fitted with new headstocks, couplings and buffers, and sold to an unknown buyer in 1910. Eighteen other vehicles were certainly sold but details have not survived. The rest were presumably left for some time before being broken up. The fate of perhaps the most interesting of all of the rolling stock, the Advertising Car, is also unknown.

One of the A.N.D.R. passenger cars, however, was saved at the very last moment. Number 3 (A.N.D.R.), when passing to the G.W.R. became number 64, eventually being used as a holiday chalet in a park near Totnes. In 1985, David Rouse of the Great Western Rolling Stock Fund discovered that the coach was to be destroyed, and arrangements were made with the curator of the Welsh Industrial Museum at Cardiff for transfer and eventual restoration to A.N.D.R. condition. On December 5th 1985, the last survivor of two great travelling shows was lifted from its long days of obscurity in Devon to be moved to Wales and take its rightful place in history.

Employing six hundred men in its best years, the firm of W.R. Renshaw & Co. ceased trading, the Phoenix Works and the winter quarters being sold in 1911. The winter quarters were sold to Twyfords Ltd., the well known sanitary manufacturers, who duly had the site converted for their business. The grounds remained until the early 1950s, when they were demolished and a multi-story block built.

## WAGONS

Many of the road vehicles remained with the show for the duration of the life of the Wild West. Some were plain box wagons for carrying anything from canvas to confectionery, most painted in the show's yellow livery, but others were more specialised. These included the ticket wagon, the band-wagons, the vehicles which housed the electric lighting equipment and the range wagon, used for cooking. These were hauled by four, six and eight horse teams which could be doubled up when conditions dictated. Often, bad weather meant muddy fields where wagons could sink up to their axles, and pulling power would be needed to extricate them. Some of the utility wagons, such as those carrying the framework, poles and seating were thirty-five feet long, and very heavy. Lighter vehicles such as the ticket wagon needed only a two-horse team. When loaded upon the railway flat cars, the box wagons were covered by tarpaulins to protect the contents from the weather, and once secured, became the responsibility of the Master of Transportation.

The electric lighting equipment was considered very modern and interesting enough to be included in the street parades. Although few people really understood what it was that they were looking at, the machinery was enigmatic enough to be shown off. The lighting vehicle was drawn by a six-horse team, and was an open affair showing the large brass boiler and flywheels etc. An attendant usually sat with the driver and there was also a large box carrier at the rear, in which another sometimes travelled. The three-foot steering wheels were dwarfed by the two rear ones, twice as big to bear the load of the rear mounted boiler.

The ticket office was a fairly simple wagon with large decorated wheels and a three section, semi-circular transom, with hatches from which business was done. It was painted deep yellow with florid lettering announcing, 'Buffalo Bill's Wild West' on the sides, and 'Ticket Office' on each section of the transom, below the hatches. New ticket wagons were introduced over the years. The band wagons were very elaborate, with much sculptural adornment, scrollwork and sham organ pipes, in the manner of a calliope (mobile steam organ). Pulled by a team of eight draught horses, the band sat on the top of the vehicles. Again, the wheelbase was quite high to give a more imposing look to the wagon, and the front steering wheels were normally slightly smaller than the rear ones.

Mention must be made here of the legendary Jake Posey who drove for Buffalo Bill, and previously for Barnum & Bailey. Posey was renowned for his handling of the 'forty horse hitch' while employed with the famous circus. This was a grouping of ten rows of great Percherons hitched four abreast. Posey began with sixteen animals, adding four more at a time as he became familiar with them. Each pole horse weighed two thousand pounds and with one rein to each pair, the arrangements were known as a military hitch. Posey held the lead rein between his thumb and forefinger with the other reins distributed between his other fingers. So long was the train of horses that the lead animal was eighty yards from the driver, but knowing each horse by name, he could control them by voice. Should one not respond, however, helpers were positioned along the outside to get the horses' attention by throwing pebbles at their flanks.

As Posey (with B&B) navigated the narrow streets of King's Lynn during the street parade, a policeman saw the lead horses coming towards him around a corner. On the corner was a public house. The lead horses were trained to take corners at speed in order to allow those following to be clear before the whole team straightened up. In this way, curbs and any other obstructions could be cleared. The policeman, not aware of the situation, stepped out and seized the two lead horses (Fritz and Paul), thinking they were runaways, causing the following rows to pile up. One of the circus men, Tom Lynch, rushed to try to keep the horses moving but was kicked, and the front hub of the leading wagon wheel crashed into and came away with the pub's glass window. Many of the pub's customers were standing behind the window watching the parade and some were carried away in the debris, but luckily with little injury. Oddly, the landlord's name was 'James Bailey', but was of no relation to the circus owner, and after the show's legal adjuster settled with him, he changed the name of the establishment to the 'Forty Horse Hitch'.

Later, when Posey drove for Buffalo Bill, and the Wild West also visited King's Lynn, Cody returned with Jake for a drink with the landlord.

## AND SHIPS

Most areas of research for this book go back almost a century, and it is not therefore surprising that detailed information on some of the ships used by the Wild West has been lost or destroyed over the years. That which follows has been put together from a variety of sources, both conventional and otherwise, in order to give as full an account as possible of the individual vessels involved. Although there is little known in some instances, researches continue.

### S.S. STATE OF NEBRASKA
This steamship was the vessel which brought the Wild West to England for the American Exhibition in London in 1887. Built in Glasgow, in 1880 by London & Glasgow Irnwks. Ltd., she

was owned by Joseph A. Allen of the same city. She weighed 2480 tons and her measurements were: length 331 feet, width 36.3 feet, and depth of hold was 28.6 feet. L.&G.I. were eventually absorbed by Harland & Wolff.

In 1887, the State of Nebraska was commanded by Captain Braes, and was of the State Line. No doubt the vessel was chosen for her name, Nebraska being close to the heart of Cody, and when she left her berth in New York on 31st March, carrying the Wild West, the cowboy band played 'The Girl I Left Behind Me'. The manifest included 38 steerage passengers, 97 Indians, 180 horses, 18 buffalo, 10 mules, 10 elk, 5 Texas steers, 4 donkeys and 12 deer. The buffalo would not be driven aboard over the gangplanks, and had to be cajoled into cargo nets and then lifted onto the ship by steam winches. Steers were penned forward and horses aft, and during the twelve day voyage, only one draught horse was lost.

Also aboard were western paintings which would be hung next to the Wild West grounds at the American Exhibition.

## S.S. LINCOLN
Built originally by Earles of Hull in 1883 for the Manchester, Sheffield and Lincoln Railway Company, the S. S. Lincoln, together with the Elzina (Elzino) conveyed the Wild West from Belgium to Grimsby after its tour of the European mainland. The Lincoln carried mainly passengers and baggage in this instance. She was a fairly small ship of only 1075 tons, with a length of 251.5 feet, width of 32.2 feet and a depth of hold of 15.8 feet. She was registered at the Port of Grimsby, Lincolnshire.

## S.S. ELZINA (ELZINO)
There is a certain amount of uncertainty regarding information available on this vessel. While the newspaper reports of the period refer to her as the Elzino, she seems in fact to be the Elzina. Perhaps this is due to simple reporting errors, or some difficulty in reading the name of the ship. The reader will see in another chapter that the vessel was held in quarantine in the Humber estuary for a week and therefore, unable to actually see the ship for themselves, reporters would be likely to hear her

name second hand. She was built in 1858, and previously named the Eliza Constance. In 1891, when she was employed by the Wild West to bring most of the stock, including the quarantined buffaloes, to England, she was owned by M. Matthys of Antwerp. Oddly, the Eliza Constance does not appear on Lloyds Register or any other major reference sources.

## S.S. SWITZERLAND
This ship was a screw steamer built in 1873 by Palmers & Co. of Jarrow, with a total weight displacement of 2806 tons. Specifications were: length 329.4 feet, width 38.6 feet and depth of hold 30.5 feet. She was at the time of charter by Buffalo Bill, part of the Red Star Line. Construction was more on the design of what we now think of as twentieth century vessels, with a high central superstructure, one funnel and a mast fore and aft. She was powered by two independent, direct acting cylinders giving 290 horsepower. The ship was built of iron with seven bulkheads, was double bottomed with two main decks. Sailing from Philadelphia to Antwerp, she was chartered by Cody in his return to the Wild West as it began its European tour in 1891. This was after his involvement with the 'Ghost Dance' uprising, and brought with him many of the Indians who had taken part, and who had been given special permission to travel with the Wild West in a short European tour. They were at this time considered as official prisoners of war. The 10th edition of the programme states that several of the Indians suffered from sea-sickness during the crossing of the Atlantic, and they referred to the ship as a 'floating house'. In fact some had died in the crossing, (see chapter 'Indians').

## S. S. MOHAWK
No historical details or specifications of this ship are at present available. It is certain that she was an American liner and conveyed the Wild West from London's Tilbury Docks on October 14th 1892, via the North Sea and the English Channel, to Jersey City. Due to the size of the show, any vessel used would be chartered for its sole use for the duration of the voyage, and around 1892, the cost would be in the region of $30,000.

*A photograph reproduced from the programme showing a ship used by the Wild West, which could only be the S.S. Switzerland.*

## PERSIAN MONARCH

This is by far the most interesting vessel, from the point of view that we seem to know far more about her than any other connected with the Wild West. It was upon this ship that the show departed from Hull in 1888, and she was utilised again later. Details of her adventures when leaving the port of Hull in 1888 can be found in the chapter 'Wondrous Wild'.The Persian Monarch was one of three 'Monarchs', built by Archibald McMillan and Son of Dumbarton, Scotland, in yard number 227, and launched on 8th September 1880. She was a single funnelled, four masted, barque rigged, screw steamer with four decks. Her measurements were; length 360 feet, width 43.1 feet and depth of hold (from tonnage deck to ceiling) 16.6 feet. The vessel was driven by a pair of compound, direct acting, inverted cylinders of 46" and 87" respectively, with a 57" stroke giving a maximum of 500 horsepower. These were made by David Rowan of Glasgow in 1880, the year that the Persian Monarch was built. Her engine room measured a length of sixty feet. Weight distribution for the ship was: weight under tonnage deck 1855.64 tons, closed in spaces above tonnage deck 1029.38 tons and roundhouse 38.4 tons, a gross tonnage of 3922.78.Clinker built on an iron framework with an elliptic stern, the Persian Monarch had no head and no galleries, and her first owner was the Royal Exchange Shipping Company of London. She was eventually sold to Thos. Wilson & Sons of Hull, but was probably chartered by that company before actual purchase. The date of her registration in Hull was 3rd March, 1891, although she was registered in the name of Arthur Wilson on 24th March, 1890. The bill of sale was dated 2nd March, 1891, with Charles James Newbauld appointed as manager for the ship. While flying the Wilson pennant, the Persian Monarch was painted in 1899 by one of the Jacobsen family, marine artists of New York, and the painting is now in possession of the Buffalo Bill Historical Museum, and must have been commissioned while the vessel was under charter to Wilson & Sons. Sometime in 1893, the ship ran aground off Fire Island, New York, but other mishaps were yet to come.The Wilson Line was established by Thos. Wilson and traded as an independent company under his sons until 1916 when it was sold to Sir John Ellerman, becoming Ellerman's Wilson Line. The Hull registry for the Persian Monarch closed when sold to I. J. Merritt, an American. A letter dated 22nd June, 1894 from the British Consul General in New York confirmed the details and was countersigned by the Registrar of Shipping.

The other 'Monarchs' built by McMillans were the Egyptian Monarch and the Lydian Monarch, built to the same specifications as the Persian Monarch and also originally owned by the Royal Exchange Shipping Company. The Lydian Monarch was also known as the Lydia. Lydia was an ancient kingdom in Asia Minor and so she was named in keeping with her sisters. These vessels were also eventually owned by the Wilsons of Hull, and although have no apparent connection with Buffalo Bill's Wild West, the reader may be interested in their fate. The Egyptian Monarch was renamed the Ohio in 1895. She was sold to F. J. Bardens of Kobe, Japan, early in 1904 and was wrecked off Korea on October 26th in that year. The Lydian Monarch was renamed the Ontario in 1895 and sold in 1902 to J. J. King and Sons Ltd. of Garstang, near Liverpool. She was broken up in 1903. In researching the ships, another Monarch was discovered with an unusual and possibly relevant connection. This was the Assyrian Monarch, the ship that was chartered to take the famous African elephant 'Jumbo', to America after being purchased by Barnum. Examination of a photograph of this vessel shows her to be virtually the same specification as the other Monarchs and a pennant, closely resembling the Wilson Line's, flies at her stern, although no definite connection can be established. The Assyrian Monarch was (like the S. S. Lincoln) built by Earles of Hull in 1880 for the Royal Exchange Shipping Company, (as were the other Monarchs). In 1887 she was sold on to J. & A. Allen of Glasgow for the New York run, and eventually broken up in 1901. Returning to the Persian Monarch, we find that sometime between 1894 and 1898 she was resold to Charles Flint & Co. converted to sail and renamed the Mayflint. Rigged at Newport News, she had made several long voyages and had her share of troubles. In 1899, she sailed from Bayonne, New Jersey, bound for Hong Kong with a cargo of case oil. Her skipper was Captain R. Banfield, apparently new to the Mayflint. Built as a steamship with ballast tanks fitted accordingly, she did not respond well under sail alone and had many 'peculiarities', according to crew reports. Not all of the sailors, however, were experienced and the ship was soon in difficulties in a freshening westerly wind. Top gallants and light fore-and-aft sails were taken in and later the upper topsails were reefed. For two days the ship's crew fought to sustain her in heavy weather. Broaching to with the wheel hard up, the main lower topsail sheet broke free and was threatening more damage to the rigging and superstructure housings. Captain Banfield and two men were struggling with the double-wheel in the wheelhouse, and as the first mate entered, told him "No use, Mister. She's hard up. Brace the foreyards". According to the first mate's recollections, the ship was 'shaking aloft and shipping water from the break of the poop to the fo'c'slehead.' Spare spars from

previous hard times were used to reinforce the number two hatch but even so, ring bolts were torn from the deck. Eventually, as the weather improved a little and it grew light, only the mizzen topsheet was holding, two men were injured and a third missing. The crew began clearing away wreckage and began hauling in gear that was trailing over the sides. One man was discovered trapped in rigging on the lee side of the ship and was released by the mate, sliding along the rail with a knife between his teeth. As the wind slackened, the Mayflint listed to port by fifteen degrees and it was discovered that the cargo had shifted. Checking the sail locker for spare canvas, the mate found the manifest to be dangerously short. Entry of the findings were entered into the ship's log and after some discussion, it was decided to return to New York. A donkey boiler was used to pump out the lee ballast tanks in order to right the vessel but this was only partly successful. Three days later, the Mayflint was off Sandy Hook and brought into Gravesend by the tug, Wallace B. Flint. Pig Iron was brought on board and slid down wherever possible on the weather side, and duly the ship was on an even keel. Re-sailed and supplied, the Captain changed his mind again and set sail for Hong Kong once more, arriving there 179 days later, having developed a starboard list. In Hong Kong, six men deserted before the vessel put into dry dock at Whampoa Dockyard, Kowloon. Here, new bilge pumps and a large water-tube boiler were fitted. Later bound for Seattle, out of the Philippines, the ship could not make headway northwards and signalled the US transport, General Grant, to report her turning south. She ran aground on a reef in the Gilolo Passage but managed to break free by pumping out the port ballast tanks, and waiting to be floated off. Finally reaching Seattle, the Mayflint was sold again and sailed for San Francisco with 5,200 tons of coal. On the return to Seattle, she entered San Francisco harbour once more, and fouled the bows of the United States Battleship, Iowa. The warship was fitted with a ram stem and badly damaged the Mayflint. So ended the life of the ship upon which Buffalo Bill had crossed the Atlantic on more than one occasion.

Prior to leaving with the Wild West from Hull, on 5th May, 1888, the Persian Monarch underwent minor refitting at that port. Newspaper reports show her arriving in Hull from New York on April 14th in time to complete the work and embark the show. Cody and Salsbury planned to take the Wild West into Europe in

1893, appearing at the Exposition Universale, and again used the Persian Monarch to take them there, landing at Le Havre.

## AND WINGS

While researching the visits of Buffalo Bill's Wild West to Yorkshire and Lincolnshire, another interesting character came to light, and while having no direct connection with the latter is deserving of mention for the following reasons. The man was American, had been involved with his own western show, and was also named Colonel Cody.

He was Samuel Franklin Cody. While no relative of Buffalo Bill, he dressed and resembled the original Cody down to his goatee beard and broad brimmed hat. We must not however decry Samuel Franklin Cody, for his exploits in other areas were certainly as worthy as those of his namesake.

Born on the outskirts of Fort Worth, Texas, in 1862, Samuel Franklin came to England in the 1890's, producing western extravaganzas in the music halls with titles such as 'The Klondike Nugget'. His parents had been immigrants from Ulster, but had found settling in America difficult, moving frequently from place to place. The young Samuel had travelled to the Klondike in the days of the gold rush but had not proved a successful prospector, and consequently turned to the stage in order to support himself. During this period, Buffalo Bill's star was rising and Samuel saw the advantage of having the same name, riding a white horse and wearing thigh-length boots. Part of his act, like the other Cody, included feats of marksmanship and it was said that he could drive in a nail at fifty feet.

Once in England, Samuel continued to play the part of the westerner, both on and off the stage. Eventually his interests encompassed flight, and in particular kites, which he was convinced were of use from a military point of view. After many experiments, some of which involved lifting a man by kite, Samuel Franklin managed to interest the Navy in the theory and was given money, workshops and the use of a naval vessel to expand his ideas. Gradually, the Royal Navy lost interest in his kites. It was around this time that the Wright brothers made their first flight at Kittyhawk and Samuel's interests were turning

towards the aeroplane. He was also partly responsible for the planning and construction of the first British airship.

On 16th May, 1909, Samuel Franklin Cody made the first successful, officially recorded flight in Great Britain at Laffin's Plain, now Farnborough. Five months later, from October 15th to 23rd, he took part in the first British Aviation Meeting at the Doncaster racecourse. During the meeting Samuel Franklin became a naturalised British subject, and signed the papers using the back of a course official as a desk. During the meeting, his plane was damaged and spent much time under repair.

Always aware of the importance of publicity, Samuel maintained some connections with the travelling show, on one occasion inviting Indians to fly with him on one of his aeroplanes. When the King inspected one of his flying machines, he mistakenly referred to Samuel as 'Colonel' Cody, a title which he then adopted for the rest of his life. Despite this, like Buffalo Bill, Samuel Franklin Cody was looked upon as a thoroughly decent fellow, liked and admired by all who knew him. He was killed in a flying accident in 1913.

*The 'other' Cody. Samual Franklin Cody, shown at the first British Aviation Meeting at the Doncaster Racecourse.*

## BUSINESS, BULLETS AND BUFFALO

### 1891

*Return of the Wild West. Landing at Grimsby and problems with quarantine. Gunslingers and tragedy in the arena.*

In 1889, Cody again crossed the Atlantic with the Wild West for a tour of Europe, opening at the Grand Exposition in Paris. Western dress became the fashion, from buckskins to Stetsons and when popcorn was introduced that year, five tons were sold on the showgrounds. Moving on to play many of the European capitals, Buffalo Bill was wined and dined by many Royal personalities and in Italy, while the show was encamped in the Coliseum, Cody and his staff (including the Indians), were given an audience with Pope Leo XlII. In Germany, high ranking officers of the military were ordered by the Kaiser to note carefully the way that the Wild West was organised, in its movement by rail and the feeding of so many men and horses. Sometimes up to forty officers of the Prussian Guard would stand with notebooks busy, noticing each worker's position while working and the lay of every rope and wagon. Years later, during World War One, the mobile field kitchens and supply trains of the German Army would reflect what they had learned from the Wild West.

*Buffalo Bill & Cowboys. A post card sold on the showground during the Wild West's tour of France.*

The 1891 season began in Strasbourg on 19th April, and after visiting many of the major towns that were served by the railways, the show then crossed into Belgium on 28th May, enthralling the crowds of Brussels and Antwerp. While in Belgium, an Indian named 'Hard-to-Hit' had discharged a firearm accidentally and wounded himself in the knee. Such incidents were common in the daily life of the Wild West, but more serious events were just ahead. Much had happened since Buffalo Bill had sailed from Hull aboard the Persian Monarch, three years before. Back home, he had become involved in the fight against abysmal conditions on the reservations by the Indians, the uprising known as the 'Ghost Dance' or the 'Messiah Craze'. This culminated in the bloody massacre of Wounded Knee, which is briefly accounted in the chapter, 'Indians'. Sitting Bull was dead, killed by Indian Police, but on a brighter note, Annie Oakley was back with the show. During one performance, Annie had shot a lighted cigarette from the mouth of the Kaiser, and later, after the outbreak of the First World War, said that she would be happy to repeat the performance, if the German Ruler was willing. The Kaiser's reply was not recorded!

*An artist's impression of Wild West cowboys repulsing an attack by Indians. A postcard sold on the showground during the tour of France.*

An outbreak of pleuro-pneumonia in Germany, a disease that affects ruminant animals, cast serious doubts upon the show being able to continue on to England. The rest of the company performed as normal in Belgium; Brussels from 28th April until 11th June and Antwerp from 12th to 17th June, but possibly due to the refusal of entry by the Belgian authorities, the nineteen buffalo were despatched directly to England via the S. S. Elzino (Elzina), leaving Antwerp and arriving at the port of Grimsby in Lincolnshire. While in Germany, a telegram was sent by the Wild West to the directors of the Manchester, Sheffield and Lincolnshire Railway Company, explaining the situation. The M.S. and L would provide the railway support for the show upon landing in England. A deputation of directors, together with their General Manager, Mr. Pollit, quickly set up a meeting with Mr. Chaplin, the senior official of the port's Agricultural Department, asking him to relax the quarantine rules.

Such was the charisma of Cody, and the high profile of the Wild West, that top company officers would act on their behalf to ensure the success of the tour. Doubtless too of course, that a considerable sum was at stake should the show not need to avail itself of the facilities of the M.S. & L., but the fact that a full deputation of directors was involved seems to suggest that Cody may have met these men before. It is possible that the Wild West had used the company at some stage during the tour of 1887/8.

*A ticket to the Columbian Exposition in Chicago 1893 where the Wild West was playing.*

*A photograph reproduced from the 'Rough Rider' giving a unique view of the Wild West showgrounds.*

Knowing that the show was scheduled to commence in Leeds on the 20th, Chaplin agreed to give the matter some thought, and eventually gave in, making some concessions, providing that he could remain within the spirit of the regulations laid down by the Agricultural Department. The advertisements were already being posted. The brightly coloured posters were all around Leeds, heralding the coming of the big show. A cancellation would now mean considerable embarrassment, as rarely had a performance been missed. The newspaper adverts boasted of 'two performances daily, rain or shine', and indeed, years later in 1908 in Trinidad, Colorado, the Wild West would play through snow in an early September blizzard. Even Buffalo Bill, however, could not fight pleuro-pneumonia. By 10th June a decision was made and the Board of Agriculture wrote to the various interests connected with the show, informing of their judgement. The Board would inspect the stock aboard the Elzino, and afterwards would allow non-ruminant animals and other cargo to be disembarked. The buffalo would have to remain aboard the vessel, at anchor in the Humber estuary, for a period of seven days from leaving Antwerp, whereupon another inspection would be made by the Grimsby Port Sanitary Authority's veterinary, Mr. Loft. At that time, providing all was well, the animals would be allowed on shore. This was very reasonable, as it was not unknown for port authorities of the day to insist upon considerably longer quarantine periods. In past years, even gifts of livestock to Queen Victoria had been confined for three months. The Board also instructed that all remaining fodder and manure must be thrown overboard prior to the Elzino finally landing the Bison. A reporter from the Grimsby News went out to the S.S. Elzino on Tuesday 17th, but was not allowed on board, then on 18th June, Mr. Loft was rowed out to the ship. After boarding and exchanging brief pleasantries with the captain, and accompanied by a cowboy charged with the care of the buffalo while on board ship, he climbed down to give the final inspection. Among the animals were two calves born in Berlin, and doubtless to Dr. Loft's unease, one very big bull bison which was (according to the Hull Daily Mail) stated to have already killed three men. A similar statement in the Grimsby News the next day revised the number of the bull's apparent victims to just two. There is no evidence to support the fact that any fatalities occurred and such an animal would certainly have been destroyed. The publicity for such a story however, would pay dividends at the box-office. The last performance of the Wild West in Belgium had been on 17th June, then sailing from Antwerp amidst cheering crowds. At four o' clock on the morning of the 18th, the steamship 'Lincoln', specially fitted out to accommodate the Wild West, and also owned by M.S. & L. Railway Company, eased into her berth in the Grimsby Docks with the main body of the show.

Immediately the work of disembarking began, beginning with the heavy draught horses which would haul most of the equipment and props onto the waiting trains. The word spread quickly and the people of Grimsby began to arrive to watch the unloading. In the meantime, some of the Indians had left the ship and were taking refreshments at a local café. Not surprisingly, before too long a crowd had gathered to view the unusual visitors, but the Indians were now used to gaping faces and hardly bothered to return the glances. The reporter from the Grimsby News had mixed feelings about them:-

'These Indians are magnificent men, some of them standing a good deal over six feet, and dressed in their fancied colours they are a sight to make even an Englishman jealous. We noticed that when they walked, as they did do, about half past ten o' clock to Mr. Revell's refreshment room for breakfast, that the women,

seven in number, did nearly all of the hard work in the line of carrying their various belongings. The way some of these fine men were stained was very interesting, but while the artificial colouring highlights their natural fierce look, it does not enhance their personal beauty. . .

Very few, if any, speak English; they are getting old and care not to change the tone of their voices, nor do they tend to be too friendly towards the Englishman, for we remember when they were in London they slightly prejudiced the English people against themselves.'
The Grimsby News, 19th June 1891.

The reporter continued to describe other impressions of the morning. . .

'All the morning, Americans, cowboys, Indians, Negroes, and if we are not mistaken, Germans, occupied the docks during the time their baggage was being examined by the Custom authorities, and the characteristic nasal twang of the Yankee was to be heard from four in the morning till noon.'
The Grimsby News, 19th June 1891.

The buffalo were landed that day and a complete itinerary of Dr. Loft's findings dispatched to the Department of Agriculture. Many sightseers had gathered on Tower Island to await the docking of the Elzino, and at three in the afternoon it hove into the lock pit of the dock. There was a short delay while formalities were dealt with, then the buffalo were finally unloaded by means of a wooden horsebox being swung over the side of the ship by a crane. Three mounted cowboys then drove the animals down a prepared gangway into nearby slaughterhouse pens, and in such a manner the whole herd was unloaded in less than an hour. The animals were housed in the foreign cattle depot at the Grimsby docks to await the journey to Leeds. After confinement aboard the S.S. Elzino, this must have been a great improvement in the conditions extended to the buffalo.

A special room was prepared containing sulphur fumes and

carbolic acid, through which all who had been in contact with the bison had to pass. With this final act, the conditions of the Board of Agriculture were satisfied, the bison at last cleared to continue on to their English debut in Leeds. The show's general manager, John. M. Burke expressed his gratitude at the courtesy and facilities extended to the Wild West by the port of Grimsby in dealing with the buffalo.

While the unloading and the scenes concerning the buffalo were being enacted, the Indians, now having left Mr. Revell's establishment, waited around the dock until their turn to board the train, taking their ease laying on packing crates and sacks. They drew by far the greatest interest with their feather knots and painted faces, and the dock police were forced to keep onlookers moving in order to allow work to continue without hindrance.

After receiving immediate medical treatment for his wound in Antwerp, it had been decided to send 'Hard-to-Hit' directly to Leeds rather than leave him in Belgium. He had arrived on the 18th and was conveyed by train, and then ambulance to the General Infirmary.

In all, three trains were needed to transport the Wild West to Leeds. The M.S. & L. had provided cattle trucks, passenger cars and other assorted wagons, forty-seven in all. Into fourteen of the cattle trucks, 128 of the high bred horses were established, and the four big mules which pulled the Deadwood Stagecoach. At intervals of about one hour they left, bound for the Wellington Station in Leeds, first the majority of the human cargo arriving at one o'clock, then the livestock at two, and finally the remainder of the props and equipment later in the day. The buffalo would remain in isolation, arriving last of all.

The playbills highlighting the city's walls and hoardings were as colourful and wildly descriptive as ever. . .

NEW ARENA,
CARDIGAN FIELDS, LEEDS
An Educative and Instructive Festival In History and

Amusements for the Midland Counties WILL OCCUR AT LEEDS COMMENCING JUNE 20, 1891
In the First and Only Appearance in this Section of the MAMMOTH EXHIBITION of the Century

THE ORIGINAL
BUFFALO BILL'S
(Col. W. F. Cody)
WILD WEST

The World Reknowned AMERICAN SCOUT and Indian Aggregation depicting Grandly Natural and Realistic Scenes on the FAR FRONTIER of the UNITED STATES with 200 Indians, Scouts, Cowboys, Mexican Vaqueros, Riflemen, Western Girls, 200 Animals, Horses, Mules, Ponies, Wild Buffaloes, Steers &c.

Everything NATURAL, NO GUILDING, NO HUMBUG! Its Standing, Class, and Merit as the Novelty of the Age in Originality, Endorsed in London, New York, Paris, Rome &c.
IN FACT BY ITS LATE TRIUMPHANT TOUR Of Continental Europe! Plain, Primitive, Colossal in all Arrangements. Largest Arena ever used necessary - Picturesque Camp. Natural Life. Wild Horses. Cowboy Buck Riders. Racing. Lassoing. Shooting Feats by Men and Women. Stage Coach Attack. War Dances. Picturesque Indian Village and Pioneer Camp. THRILLING!

MIMIC BATTLE SCENES
By THOSE WHO HAVE BEEN THERE!
Covered Stands for 3,000 Persons. Seats for 8,000 Persons.
4,000 Seats for one Shilling!

LIFE, LIGHT, AIR, HEALTH AND COMFORT
For a Summer Afternoon or Night,
With a Practical
Three Years' Tour in Western America
In a Two Hours' Entertainment at Home!

This is the same Company that was at London, under the same

management, Messrs. CODY & SALSBURY, all under the lead of the original COL. W. F. CODY, "BUFFALO BILL" and has with its Indians some of the most celebrated amongst the 'Friendlies' and 'Hostiles' of last winter's campaign in Dakota, notably "Kicking Bear", "No Neck", "Yankton Charlie", "Long Wolf", "Lone Bull", "Black Heart", "Scatter", "Revenge", "Big Wolf" and "Short Bull". Prices: 1s, 2s, 3s, and 4s.

Two Performances daily

3 p.m. and 8 p.m. Rain or Shine. BRILLIANT NIGHT
ILLUMINATIONS

THE EVENT OF A LIFE-TIME IT NEVER RETURNS

For CHEAP EXCURSIONS see RAILWAY
ANNOUNCEMENTS

The posters and flyers were printed by Stafford & Co. of Netherfield, Nottingham, whose credit was printed on the bottom. Some carried illustrations by J. Hopkin Koln, taken from the current programmes sold on the showground, and nearly all showed a head and shoulders portrait of Buffalo Bill.

Cody had left for Leeds earlier, with Salsbury and some of his staff, to establish himself at the Queens Hotel. This would not have necessarily been a purely selfish gesture as it was important to capitalise on his public relations powers in the best interests of the show. Who better to publicise the Wild West than Buffalo Bill?

The tactic worked well as usual, for in the afternoon a flurry of reporters, and interested and involved personages waited on the great scout. The Yorkshire Evening Post representative compared Cody's looks favourably with the images on the posters, pasted around the city, noting his fine physique and genial manners, 'with only a hint of an American accent'. Rumours had been circulating that the show was not the huge concern that had played on the continent but this was quickly scotched. As if to prove his point, Cody played his next regular trump card by inviting a party of notables, including the press, to lunch the following day at the showground on the city's Cardigan Fields. The publicity machine was rolling.

As usual, the de-training was faultless and fluid, and no doubt the line of wagons rolling through the town drew much attention. The weather had not been good, but on Friday 19th June, 1891, the sun shone brightly. At Cardigan Fields the canvas city was erected once more, awaiting the thousands who would flock through the ticket barriers in the days to come. Behind the backdrop of the main arena, the Indian encampment was set up, close to the River Aire. It is interesting to note that the Indians expressed their reluctance to bathe in the Aire due to the obvious pollution of the river.

Those who arrived a little early for the pre-arranged lunch at the show site wandered around the teepees admiring the colourful craftwork of the squaws and occasionally passed a polite remark.

Entering the dining tent, the party sat with Buffalo Bill dominating the proceedings. With him were Nate Salsbury, Major John Burke and other members of the general staff. The health of the Queen and the Prince of Wales were duly toasted and then they drank to the health of Buffalo Bill, who acknowledged the sentiment. About this time, possibly prompted by the gentlemen of the press, an invitation was extended to several of the Chiefs among the Indians, and to the delight of the guests, it was accepted.

Those who came to the marquee to join the gentlemen of Leeds included Plenty Wolves, No Neck, Kicking Bear and Black Heart. Also there was Short Bull, said to have been one of the leaders of the recent Sioux uprising, and considered a 'Messiah' by his contemporaries. Salsbury told the Yorkshire Evening Post reporter that Short Bull had 'bluffed sixty five million Americans by causing such commotion in the United States'. Another in the company was Long Wolf, whose true Indian name was 'Schoongamoneta Hoska'. Long Wolf was seen more as a guide and philosopher than a War Chief, much in the same light as Sitting Bull, and it was said that he had advised against making a war against the whites as they were too strong. He would never see the plains again.

As the Indians entered, there was a bustle of handshakes all around, and it became quite obvious to the guests that these native Americans were considered a vital and essential part of the show, and were treated so. Most journalists present commented on their marked 'Roman-like' features and proud bearing, and skilled use of the knife and fork. Although 'firewater' was freely available, the reporter from the Yorkshireman would later express his surprise that the Sioux drank only lemonade and soda water, and instead of the peace pipe, preferred cigarettes.

After lunch was done, several of the Chiefs were prompted to give speeches and express their thoughts of the Wild West and its travels. They did so eloquently, surprising some of the listeners with dry humour, especially Kicking Bear. No Neck gave a graphic account of the recent rising, and also present was little Johnny Burke No Neck, a young Indian boy who had been found on the battlefield of Wounded Knee, lying for days without food or water.

Many of the Indians sent a good proportion of their earnings home to their families, Cody keeping a bank for them and regularly sending the money back to the United Sates on their behalf. Although many, indeed up to the present day, would criticise and berate Cody in his treatment of the Indians in the show, there are many instances to illustrate his kindness and consideration. It is, however, for the readers to seek out the references and decide for themselves.

The lunch ended, speeches made and National Anthems sung, the visitors were then invited to inspect the stables. Here was separate accommodation for draught horses and the show horses, and the guests were shown the latter, where more than a hundred animals were housed. The main interest was in the bucking broncs with names such as 'Misery Mike', 'Indigestion', 'Hard Scrabble', and 'Dynamite'. This last animal was true to his name and Cody offered ten pounds, Sterling, to any of the reporters who might wish to try to ride him. All declined.

After wishing Buffalo Bill and Nate Salsbury the best of luck, the guests left them to complete their preparations. They would be back to view the Wild West performances in the days to come.

A week later, an incident occurred which showed the margin between the westerners and their hosts. One journalist had incurred the displeasure of one of the riders in the show by expressing criticism in his column. Why and for what reason we can only imagine, but that Saturday evening, the cowboy strapped on his pistols and hunted the streets of Leeds, looking for the man. Suffice to say that in the large city he did not run his quarry to ground and all ended well. An amusing incident now, but one which could have had disastrous repercussions for the Wild West.

Of the performances in Leeds, much good was written in the weekly and daily columns, especially of the big set pieces such as the attack on the settler's cabin, and the Deadwood Stage. As ever, Buffalo Bill and Annie Oakley stole much of the limelight, and the Indians in their finery and war-paint retained the most general interest. The only real criticism of the Indians was a good one, in that some observers would have liked to have seen more of their legendary skills with he bow and arrow. This is quite interesting as few references were made elsewhere to the traditional weapon of the plains warriors.

On the pasture hills, adjacent to the showground, those who could not, or would not pay the price of admission, stole a view of the proceedings, some equipped with opera glasses and telescopes.

The show played in Leeds until the night of 4th July. As the last evening performance was still in progress, the wagons were already being loaded for hauling back to the waiting trains. Many stayed away from their beds until the early hours, to catch a last lingering look at the great spectacle, leaving town. Twelve years later, it would be back, and what a show it would be.

On 5th July, the Wild West was in Liverpool and there it played until the 18th. From Liverpool it travelled on to Manchester and set up on 19th at Whalley Range, Brooke's Bar, giving its first performance there on the 20th. The main entrance was located on Stamford Street and two performances were given daily, as usual at 3 p.m. and 8 p.m., with the public allowed to walk around the encampment from 6.30 p.m. As in Leeds and elsewhere, the evening performances were illuminated with the show's own electrical generating system and some strange mood effects were created by the use of coloured filters. Tickets cost the same as in Leeds, but more for special boxes, all of which could be pre-booked at Messrs. Forsyth Bros. of 122 and 124, Deansgate.

The Wild West entertained the people of Manchester for three weeks until the 8th August. On that last Saturday in Manchester, Black Heart married a Sioux woman known as Calls-the-Name, in the presence of the whole company at the local church of St. Bride's, Trafford. Whether Black Heart or his bride were Christians is not known, and it may be that a church wedding was used to highlight the occasion. A celebration was held later at the showground and Buffalo Bill presented Black heart with a gift of clothing, and his wife with a dowry. The Parish registry (entry no. 90 by license) gives Black Heart's age as 35, a bachelor, and his profession as soldier. His father was shown as White-Eye. Calls-the-Name was 44 at the time of the marriage, her second as she was a widow, and her father's name was entered as a Chief named Smoke. Both husband, wife and witnesses made crosses as signatures on marriage documents.

The weather that Saturday had been atrocious and the last performances had gone on despite the arena being knee-deep in mud, churned by the hooves of many horses. The mud and rain made the task of dismantling the camp exceedingly difficult and the departure was delayed. Eventually, some hours late, the three trains were loaded and the show rolled back into Yorkshire, to the city of Sheffield. Prompted by the advance advertising and forward press reports, hundreds had gathered to watch the arrival of the Wild West at the Wadsley Bridge Station in Sheffield, early that Sunday morning. Originally the trains were scheduled for two, three and four o' clock, but did not arrive until 3.40 a.m., 4 a.m. and 7.35 a.m. The first train brought the light wagons, the kitchens, some stock, some of the cowboys and wranglers and the Deadwood Stagecoach. Train number two carried the remainder of the company, including the cowboy band and the Indians, and more livestock. The last train transported the bulk of the canvas and hardware which made up the shell of the camp. The weather improved slightly and despite the delay, onlookers stayed until the last wagon had been unloaded and was on the road to Owlerton, where a site was arranged at Thompson's Meadow on the Penistone Road.

The Manchester, Sheffield and Lincolnshire Company's agents in Sheffield, Messrs. Thompson, McKay and Company, instructed their officer, Mr. Jefferson, to assist with the arrangements for the de-training of the 483 people and two hundred tons of baggage. By far the main problem of the journey to the show site was the trouble given at intervals by the bucking horses, but enjoyed greatly by the crowds, no doubt. Within an hour of the arrival of the first train, the cook tent had been erected at Thompson's Meadow and breakfast prepared. Endless amounts of bacon, eggs, bread, tea and coffee, were provided and consumed by the hungry workers after the efforts of the previous day.

# BUFFALO BILL'S WILD WEST

## And Congress of Rough Riders of the World.

### Headed and Personally Introduced by

## Col. W. F. CODY, "Buffalo Bill."

Now paying a Parting Salute to Great Britain.
Will positively never be seen here again. See it NOW or NEVER.

*THREE SPECIAL TRAINS.*    *1,300 MEN and HORSES.*

The World's Greatest Educational Exhibition,

EMBRACING AS IT DOES THE

# HERO HORSEMEN OF ALL NATIONS

### The only Exhibition of its kind on earth.

Native Equestrians of Europe, Asia, Africa and America, from the Canadian Mountains, the Russian Steppes, the African Deserts, the Mexican Cordilleras, the Andes and the Rocky Mountains, presenting the Equestrian Sensation of Modern Times.

**Tha Orient & Occident** RIDE **Shoulder to Shoulder** IN THE **GREAT ARENA 100** American Indians, Chiefs, Warriors, Bucks, Squaws and Papooses.

## THE GREAT Wild West — AND — Wild East

"Now United, Hand-in-Hand."

Step by step the pathfinder has recruited the globe. Note the earliest array of stirring attractions. Russian Cossacks, Bedouin Arabs, American Cowboys, South American Gauchos, Roosevelt's Rough Riders, U.S. Life Savers, Indians, Cubans, Western Girls, Mexicans, Johnny Baker, Bucking Broncos, Stage Coach, Pony Express, Emigrant Train, Scenes of Border Life on the Western American Plains.

### Imperial Japanese Troupe

— IN —
Ancient and Modern War Drill.

### THE INTREPID COWBOY CYCLIST,

IN HIS WONDERFUL
**BICYCLE LEAP THROUGH SPACE.**

"BUFFALO BILL" the Master Exponent of Horseback Marksmanship, in a Marvellous Exhibition of Shooting while riding a Galloping Horse.

The Great Programme augmented by a colossal, crowning spectacle of combat and carnage in savage warfare, introducing Eight Hundred Indians, Scouts, Soldiers and Horses, faithfully depicting the BATTLE OF THE LITTLE BIG HORN, whose Apotheosis is the Illustrious Tableau of Custer's Last Stand and Heroic Fall.

**TWO Performances Every Week Day.**

Always and Everywhere presented in uncurtailed perfection. The vast arena illuminated at night by Special Electric Light Plants.

Afternoons at 2.    Evenings at 8.    Doors open at 1 & 7 p.m.

**One Ticket Admits to all Advertised Attractions**

Prices of Admission, 1s., 2s., 3s., 4s.; Box Seats, 5s. & 7s. 6d.

Children under ten years half-price to all except the 1s. seats.

All seats are numbered except those at 1s. and 2s. No Tickets under 4s. sold in advance.

Tickets at all Prices on sale on the grounds at hours of opening, and tickets at 4s., 5s. and 7s. 6d. on sale at 9 a.m. on the day of exhibition at

*A Press Advertisement.*

Even as some began eating, others were already beginning the preliminaries of setting up the canvas city ready for the first performance. The Indians erected their teepees, watched by sightseers who admired the traditional artwork decorating the lodges. As the canvas walls of the grandstand were thrown up, little could be seen from outside, and so, many people moved into the cemetery at Wardsend, taking the best view from the bridge which was crowded for the better part of the day.

The rain of the previous day had soaked everything, making the canvas twice as heavy, and so the last of the baggage did not reach the site until ten o' clock, but by noon all was in position including the ticket office and pay-boxes. The roof of the grandstand was progressing well by skilled hands while Nate Salsbury directed the placing of the last few items.

The Sheffield Daily Telegraph noted that the Deadwood Stagecoach looked the worse for wear, but was impressed by the buffalo herd and the horses. Also to their 'taste' were the cooking arrangements for the company and the newspaper detailed the evening meal of soup, roast beef and mutton, served in the dining tent.

The next morning, part of the Wild West paraded through Sheffield where thousands lined the streets, bringing normal traffic to a standstill in the centre of town. The show went well despite inclement weather, bringing in around £1,500 per day. Then, during the afternoon performance of Friday 14th August, disaster struck at the soul of the Wild West. At the beginning of the performance, as the first band of Sioux burst into the arena one of the horses stumbled and fell against the fencing. As the animal went down the foot of the rider, Paul Eagle Star, was crushed between horse and timber causing a compound dislocation of his right ankle. He was taken directly to the Sheffield General Infirmary, situated on the Infirmary Road in the Upperthorpe area, where it was found that the foot was almost wrenched completely off. He was made as comfortable as possible, but by Saturday morning, tetanus had set in and it was necessary to amputate the limb in order to save his life. The operation was carried out that evening but the shock had been too much and Eagle Star began to deteriorate. G.C. Crager, a Sioux interpreter, who had known the Indian for only six months, travelled to the infirmary to stay with him during the operation.

The Wild West moved on to Stoke on Trent, then Nottingham, and continual telegrams enquiring as to the man's health were received at the Infirmary from the other Indians and the management.

After the operation, the Sioux expressed his gratitude to the staff of the Infirmary for their care, and the medical staff had been impressed by his fortitude despite being in much pain. Early on the morning of Monday 17th, holding Crager's hand, Paul Eagle Star murmured 'Jesus, Jesus', and died.

Paul Eagle Star was only twenty-five years old at the time of his death, and had lived on the Rosebud Agency in South Dakota, where his wife still was. Speaking English well, he had been educated at Carlisle, Pennsylvania and was popular with Cody and the rest of the staff. He had taken part in the 'Ghost dance' rising of 1890, fighting against the U.S. Army at the now infamous battle of Wounded Knee Creek, and was taken prisoner in early January, only a few months before. When Buffalo Bill had persuaded the Government to allow him to invite the 'prisoners of war' to join him in the Wild West, Eagle Star had been one of those who had agreed, probably seeing a greater freedom in touring with the show.

Immediately, a telegram was sent to the Wild West in Nottingham where the whole company was cast under a mantle of gloom. Both Cody and Salsbury were genuinely upset, and we are told by the papers of the day that Buffalo Bill was 'prostrate' and unable to travel to Sheffield to complete the funeral arrangements. Later, he sent a message thanking the resident medical staff at the Infirmary and Mr. Arthur Jackson, Mr. W. F. Favell and Mr. G.H. Shaw for their kindness and care for Eagle Star. It was said that Cody intended to present the Infirmary with a marble bust of himself in gratitude, but it is not known whether this actually came about.

An inquest was held at the Infirmary, probably on the morning of Monday 24th August, and was without doubt the strangest that Sheffield had ever witnessed. In attendance were Indians dressed in their ceremonial feathers and robes, together with the Americans in their respectful best and English gentlemen of the legal establishment. Built in 1797, the Infirmary became the Royal Infirmary in 1897. It closed as a hospital in 1980 and the original buildings are now used as general offices by the Norwich Union (at the time of writing).

Mr. D. Wightman, the Coroner presided over the inquest and also present was the American Consul in Sheffield, Mr. D. Folsom. From the Wild West were Major J. M. Burke, William Langan, the show's supply agent and interpreters Crager and J. Shangrau. The Indians, present in full ceremonial, were Kicking Bear, Black Heart, Lone Bull, and Eagle Star's cousin, Bull-Stands-Behind, who had been extremely emotional when allowed to view the body of the deceased.

*A postcard linked to the Wild West with an interesting sentiment from the sender.*

83

Crager was called as the first witness and although he had not personally seen the accident, told it as it had been related to him by the unfortunate Indian himself. Next came the House Surgeon from the Infirmary, Mr. Hugh Rhodes, who explained the medical details for the jury, and the events leading to Eagle Star's death. The Coroner told the gathering that as there was no one present that actually saw the incident, the jury should return their decision on Crager's evidence. The jury agreed and returned a verdict of accidental death. Crager then spoke again to the court, expressing 'at the wish of Colonel Cody, the gratitude of the Wild West to the staff of the Infirmary for everything that they had done for Paul Eagle Star', and that personally he, Crager, 'had never met with such kindness, nor such devotion to a stranger as he had seen at the hospital, and had the Colonel been able to come himself, would express the same sentiments'.

The Coroner then replied for the court saying that 'as Sheffielders were proud of their Infirmary, they would be pleased to hear such commendation from strangers'. After the inquest, the coffin containing the remains of the Sioux warrior was taken by hearse to the Midland Station, from where it would be taken to the West Brompton Cemetery. Cody had purchased a plot of land for the burial of another Indian when the show was at Earle's Court in 1887. Following the hearse in the first carriage were the four Indians, followed by the remainder of the mourners from the show.

At the station, a special van had been hired and attached to the regular 11.35 London train, in which was placed the coffin, accompanied by the mourners. At Nottingham, Cody arranged to have the train delayed for a short period to allow the Wild West to see their fallen comrade for one last time. The cowboy band played the 'Requiem' as the train pulled away to continue its journey, the coffin still attended by Major Burke, Crager and Bull-Stands-Behind. Paul Eagle Star was interred at the cemetery on 25th August, 1891.

Paul Eagle Star is buried in consecrated ground not far from the Fulham Road (south) entrance to the cemetery, south of the central avenue in row number four, compartment 'R', reference BR 154133.

The Wild West had moved on to Stoke on Trent, then later to Nottingham on 23rd August. As the performances continued as normal at the Trent Bridge Close (off Loughborough Road) in the West Bridgeford suburb, the wailing of the squaws could be heard in the Indian encampment, sorrow for the passing of a warrior.

*Left: Wild West Stationery.*

That year, bad weather and bad luck seemed to haunt the Wild West. August had been cold, but the street parade at eleven o' clock through the streets of Nottingham again brought traffic to a halt. Despite the portending rain, the first performance on the afternoon of 24th brought in over 7,000 spectators. Claude L. Daly, the show's pistol expert, impressed the Evening Post not only with his skill with the revolver but also his 'prodigiously developed biceps'. That day, during races between a Mexican, an Indian and a cowboy, the Mexican's horse slipped while rounding a corner, throwing its rider heavily. Though badly shaken, the man walked away from the accident with no broken bones, to the cheering of a sympathetic audience. During the afternoon performance of the last day in Nottingham, disaster almost struck once more when the timbers supporting the seating on the Loughborough Road side of the arena cracked and gave way. Annie Oakley had just begun her act when the incident occurred and it was reported that the crack of breaking timber was as loud as the gunshots, distracting the crowd. Some of the occupants of the lower seats jumped clear but most of those on one of the one-shilling stands were thrown in a mass to the ground. At first it was thought that some had been killed and injured, but this thankfully for Cody and the show, proved false. Many rushed to help Cody's men pull people clear of the wreckage, including Sergeant Wainright and other officers of the borough Police who were on duty that afternoon. The only serious injury was to thirty-five year old Owen Richardson, of 75, Lamcote Street. Oddly, he suffered only- a broken ankle. The Leicester Chronicle and Leicester Mercury named another injured man as Maurice Leavesley, a traveller of 7, Lansdowne Road, Sheffield, and that a P.C. Sturgess gave First Aid and removed the unfortunate to the Infirmary where he was detained for treatment.

The Wild West continued, and while around 8,000 watched the last performance that evening, the Indian encampment was being taken down, ready for the next stand. The show moved to Leicester, where it arrived to the usual welcome on 30th August, proceeding to the ground on the Belgrave Road, where it remained until 5th September. From 6th to the 19th September, Birmingham's Aston Lower grounds played temporary home for the show. It was rumoured at the time that many local dogs, especially the plumper ones, disappeared during the fortnight that the Indians were around. Rumours are likely to be all that they were, as the catering facilities of the Wild West were considerable and Cody would certainly have clamped down on 'clandestine raids'. Thereafter the Wild West moved southward to the following venues. . .

Cardiff
20th September to 26th September

Bristol
27th September to 2nd October

Portsmouth
3rd October to 10th October

Brighton
11th October to 17th October

Croydon
18th October to 24th October

. . . and then northward to Glasgow on 16th November where it stayed until 27th February, 1892. The strain of the European tour was now beginning to tell and Cody left Glasgow for his home in Nebraska aboard the steamer, Corean, together with some of the Indians, including Short Bull, Kicking Bear and Has-No-Horses. The ship called at Londonderry before crossing the Atlantic, docking at New York on March 18th, 1892.

The show split, part of it performing in theatres while the rest played the East End Exhibition Hall in Glasgow. An odd metamorphosis took place with the hiring of elephants and other acts more akin to the circus, but a few weeks later, Buffalo Bill was back with fresh horses, ready for the new season at Earle's Court. Now the Wild West began to change into a more cosmopolitan show, with the inclusion of a group of Cossacks under the command of Prince Ivan Rostomov Macheradse. On June 25th 1892, the Wild West was summoned to a command

*A page from the souvenir book showing exciting scenes from the Wild West.*

*Selection from children's scrapbook cuts sold at the showground.*

Buffalo Bill at full gallop shooting at balls.

*A page from the souvenir book showing exciting scenes from the Wild West.*

Indians attacking the Deadwood coach.

*Selection from children's scrapbook cuts sold at the showground.*

performance at Windsor Castle in the presence of Queen Victoria. As usual a throng of sightseers had gathered and the show was met by Major General McNeill, who informed Cody that the Queen wished to watch the entry of the Wild West into the arena from her window. Buffalo Bill, taking the lead, led the 'ride past', then put the whole company through several of its manoeuvres.

The arena faced the east terrace, in the centre of which was a small pavilion carrying the Royal Coat of Arms, and the spaces on each side were crowded with attending aristocracy. Promptly, the Queen, attired in plain black, arrived with the Princess Christian, and the Princess Beatrice and her children. When the Royal party were settled, a signal was given for the show to begin. Nate Salsbury, who had already been introduced to the Queen, stood by her during the performance explaining each act. When the show was over, he introduced the Queen to Major Burke. The Queen complimented them on the Wild West, and to Cody she gave a large gold seal with her monogram upon it, surrounded by the Royal motto. Salsbury received a beautiful scarf pin, studded with diamonds and surmounted by the Imperial Crown.

The London season ended on October 12th, 1892, and thus ended the tour of Europe, which had lasted three and a half years. Despite the troubles and sadness, none could deny the successes of the recent years. Cody was now forty-six, and feeling his years. His dark hair was becoming grizzled, but it would be ten years before the Wild West would return to England, and by then it would be snow white, transforming him into the icon that most would recognise long after his passing.

*Cody in 1893.*

88

# INDIANS...!

*Some of the personalities in the show. Cowboys, Indians, Mexicans, Vaqueros, and a little history.*

The management of the Wild West always ensured that the audience received as impressive a spectacle as could be achieved. In real life, for example, the working clothes of the cowboy were usually drab and functional but in the show they always wore bright shirts, flowing bandannas and clean, woolly chaps. In essence, the picture of the cowboy, and indeed the western scenario in general, created by Buffalo Bill was the traditional one if not the true one. The images we have in our minds of the west are directly related to the part-myth that he created with the Wild West, enhanced by Hollywood and to some extent, literature. Thankfully, since the seventies, Hollywood has seen fit to give us a more realistic view of life on the frontier in the last century. At last, the roving knight-errant cowboy with the immaculate white hat and horse has been shelved in his place with the old B-Movies. In the turn of the century industrial towns and cities of Europe, however, it was just such dash and colour that would attract the crowds, especially in the absence of modern entertainment.

Perhaps the most colourful of the ethnic groups in the Wild West were of course, the Indians. Despite their bright feathers and war paint, they were still probably the closest of any of the performers to their natural dress. The Indians were still considered to be somewhat barbaric by many audiences, who not surprisingly, were unaware of the complex social life of native Americans. Only the plains tribes were included in the show, in order to maintain the theme of the horse, and it is these warriors of the plains that have come to represent the traditional image of the Indian.

The names and events connected with the plains tribes are quite familiar to most of us, thanks to television and the movies, but few realise that these are a long historical sequence of linked events. The inevitable outcome was a chain of broken treaties, humiliation, poor treatment and eventual submission of once proud peoples such as the Cheyenne and Sioux. The real causes can be traced far back, but for the purposes of this book, and to show connections with Buffalo Bill's Wild West, we shall look to 1876 and the death of Custer.

After the Little Big Horn (known to the Sioux as the Greasy Grass), Sitting Bull took the Sioux over the border into Canada, until 1883 when the American Government, wishing to portray a magnanimous stance to the 'Indian problem', offered a free pardon to those returning to their homeland. Sitting Bull accepted and crossing back over, moved to the Standing Rock Reservation. A short time later, he joined Alvar Allen's show as the 'man who killed Custer', and although disenchanted with the affair, was still persuaded by Major John Burke to star in the Wild West for one season.

Morale among the tribes was at a low ebb, until a medicine man named Wovoka spread a new religion, which blended the old traditions with Christianity. Oddly, the origins of Wovoka's beliefs lay in Utah, where a missionary had told the Utes of the coming of a Messiah to set free the tribes and return the buffalo. Needing new hope, some of the plains Indians welcomed these beliefs and so was born the beginnings of the 'Ghost Dance' or 'Ghost Shirt' movement. Those who took up the call would wear the ghost shirt, a garment that they believed impervious to bullets. Dancing themselves into exhaustion, individuals would attempt to manifest the spirits of their ancestors. Two of the converted, Kicking Bear and Short Bull, approached the Miniconjou and Hunkpapas, spreading the word.

The American Government decided to confront Sitting Bull at Standing Rock about the new religion, fearing considerable insurrection should such an influential man be converted. Sitting Bull was interested in the Ghost Dance movement but probably still a little unsure. Buffalo Bill was back in the US, and given a mission by General Nelson Miles to go to the Sioux Chief and use his friendship with him to de-fuse the situation. For reasons which are somewhat unclear (described in the Wild West programme as jealous intrigue), Cody was intercepted and ordered to return. Had he been allowed to continue, it is possible

*Selection from children's scrapbook cuts sold at the showground.*

*Buckskin Jacket which once belonged to a Wild West performer. Buffalo Bill?*

*The centre pages of the souvenir book illustrating the attack on the emmigrant train and rescue by Buffalo Bill.*

*The back cover of the souvenir book which depicts the buffalo hunt.*

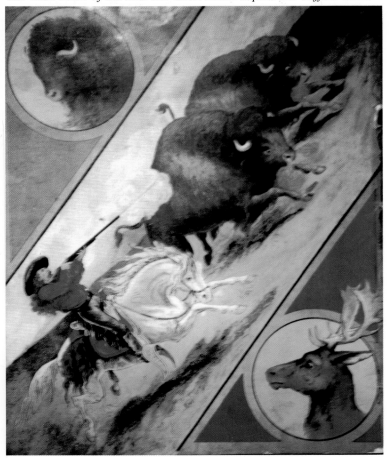

*A street parade showing Indians, Arabs and Lancers. The photograph was actually taken in Belgium.*

that Sitting Bull would have lived, and sad events, which later occurred, might have been avoided. Indian Police, commissioned by the US Army, descended upon Standing Rock on 14th December, 1890 to arrest Sitting Bull, and as some of his followers rose to defend him he was shot by Metal Breasts, one of the policemen. Upon hearing of Sitting Bull's death, the last of the Miniconjou Sioux under their chief, Bigfoot, decided to take refuge in the Badlands in order to avoid the trouble they feared would follow. It was also possible that he hoped to contact Kicking Bear and Short Bull, whom he believed to be in the area with 3,000 braves. They were pursued by a cavalry column which included men who had served with those who fell at Little Big Horn. Deciding that the Miniconjou were moving to join the Ghost Dance warriors, the cavalry overtook them on December 28th but the Sioux offered no resistance and they were headed south west by the soldiers to make camp on Wounded Knee Creek. Next morning, another four squadrons of cavalry arrived and the commanding officer, Colonel Forsyth, ordered the Sioux to give up their weapons. The cavalrymen became nervous when the Indians refused to do so, being concerned at being defenceless in such circumstances. When one brave discharged a pistol into the air as a sign of defiance, the troopers needed no other signal to open fire from all sides, accompanied by four Hotchkiss cannon.

*The aftermath of Wounded Knee. Army wagons collecting frozen Indian Corpses.*

Most of the men, including Bigfoot, were cut down at the first volley. The soldiers then fired upon the teepees housing women and children, targetting any who tried to escape, and twenty-five cavalrymen also died as a result of crossfire from their own comrades. The wounded Indians were left to die of their wounds

*Above: John Shangrau. From a photograph in the programme.*

*Left: Johnny Burke No-Neck.*

in the snow, including Bigfoot who was already suffering from pneumonia. Indian bodies were mutilated and searched for souvenirs. A few of the Sioux were found to be wearing the ghost shirts, proving to others, once and for all, that they could not stop bullets. Essentially this put an end to the Ghost Dance movement. By the end of 1890 the US census stated that the frontier no longer existed.

Among the frozen bodies, four days later, was found an Indian child still surviving, despite being without food or water. He was named Johnny Burke No-Neck (after Major Burke, who apparently found him), and also eventually found a home with Buffalo Bill's show.

Buffalo Bill needed Indians for the Wild West and names such as Kicking Bear, Short Bull, Long Wolf and others who had become well known during the hostilities were ideal. Using his influence, he inevitably helped these Sioux warriors to avoid retribution by inviting them to join him in the show's visit to England in 1892. They had been held at Fort Sheridan, and Cody managed to obtain the parole of twenty-six. John Shangrau - guide, interpreter and Government scout, was put in charge of these Indians, who were looked upon as military hostages by the authorities.

Many Indians travelled with the Wild West during its thirty-year life, mostly staying for one or two seasons before drifting into obscurity. The reader may be interested to know a little more about some of them: -

### Red Shirt (Ogila-Sa)

Billed as the Fighting Chief of the Sioux Nation, Red Shirt was born at Ogulala (also other spellings), an Indian village on the Platte river. At this time the Sioux and the Snake tribes were deadly enemies and Red Shirt's father, Little Crow, determined to raid the Snake village with fifty braves, including the young man and his uncle, Feathered Head. During the raid, Red Shirt distinguished himself as a warrior and persuaded his father to permit him to organise another raid, this time against the Pawnee. With five others he returned with fifty-seven stolen

*A recent postcard reproducing original artwork used by the Wild West.*

*Gordon Lillee alias Pawnee Bill.*

*The Deadwood coach as it appears today in the Buffalo Bill Historical Museum.*

horses, but the Pawnees followed and not only took back their own mounts but those of the Sioux while they slept.

After initial good relationships with white trappers, acts of treachery on the pat of the white men sparked off a war that

RED SHIRT
THE FIGHTING CHIEF OF THE SIOUX.

lasted six years. During this time, Red Shirt's prowess increased and after a relatively peaceful period, another war with the Pawnee ensued. Eventually in 1876, broken treaties and poor treatment by unscrupulous whites culminated in the hostilities on the Little Big Horn and the death of Custer. Then in 1877, overtures were made to Red Shirt to join Buffalo Bill and travel to England.

Red Shirt was a handsome individual with much integrity and concern for his people, and like other Indians, felt it was wise to learn as much as possible about the white man's world. He was advised by an elder, Red Cloud, not to go but with a group of carefully selected braves, remained with the Wild West for two years. While with the show in England, he was introduced to Queen Victoria, the Prince of Wales and Prime Minister, Gladstone.

### Long Wolf (Schoongamoneta Hoska)
A chief of the Ogallala Sioux, Long Wolf was with Buffalo Bill in 1892 as the head chief. On June 11th, 1892, while the show was at Earle's Court, he died at the West London Hospital and was buried at West Brompton Cemetery. After his death, Cody gave the Indian's wages to his wife, Wants.

Three of the Indians who accompanied Buffalo Bill on the journey over to England on the Switzerland died, and Long Wolf contracted pneumonia. Others in the party were Rocky Bear and Flies Above. To quote Lizzie Yellowboy Blackfeather, a descendant of Long Wolf, who recalls the stories passed down through the family. . .
"Large fish came and hit the side of the boat. The crew then thought some of the livestock had died and they searched the ship. They found an Indian woman huddled in a corner with the body of her baby. The child was buried at sea. Large fish returned, a horse died and was put overboard. When finally the ship reached London, long Wolf finally succumbed to pneumonia and Wants (his wife) was afraid to take his body back home. She thought they might have to bury him at sea".

*Long Wolf.*

Long Wolf, at the age of fifty-nine, was at the time of his death, the oldest Indian in the Wild West, and after examination by Dr. Coffin, the latter stated that the Indian's body was covered in bullet and sabre wounds. He was buried on June 13th, 1892, at ten thirty in the morning, not far from the catacombs at one end of a Greco-Roman colonnade, under a poplar tree in a grave purchased by Cody. Six Indians, together with Buffalo Bill, Nate Salsbury, John Burke, two interpreters and other members of the Wild West and London officials, attended the funeral. Knowing that his life was almost over, Long Wolf had made a drawing of a wolf and requested that it be carved upon his tombstone. In accordance with his wishes this was done and placed within a stone cross, which stands today.

The death certificate gives the cause of death as 'Senile decay - ill defined form of continued fever - nineteen days', certified by F.L. Paget M.R.C.S., and was signed by the deputy registrar, C.C. Knowles.

Considered a man of wisdom rather than a man of war, Long Wolf had counselled against a war with the white man during the Ghost Dance rising. Later, on 15th September, 1892, an Indian child named Star died at the Wild West camp at Brompton. She was the daughter of Ghost Dog and aged one year and eight months old, and was buried in the same grave as Long Wolf, under reference BR 156572. Long Wolf's reference in the cemetery is BR 156451, and both are buried in compartment 7 (3), close to the Fulham Road.

*Martha & Mary Blackfeather, Great , Great granchildren of Long Wolf at his grave in London.*

*Long Wolf's tombstone with the wolf symbol.*

Long Wolf and his wife had three children and one, Lizzie, married Grover Yellowboy. Jessie Yellowboy was then born and she later married Jim Blackfeather. It was Jessie, now in her eighties, who felt Long Wolf's spirit was not resting easy, and it is at this time that an English woman, Elizabeth Knight became involved. Elizabeth lives in Brompton and came across a book of stories and essays in her local market. One, by R.B. Cuninghame Graham, was entitled 'Long Wolf', and it briefly, if somewhat floridly, gave detail of the Indian's demise while with the Wild West. In May, 1992, co-incidentally around the time that researches for this book began, Elizabeth went to the Brompton cemetery and found Long Wolf's grave. She vowed to find the descendants of the Sioux and did so, hoping to find a way to return him to his homeland. Later, Elizabeth and her husband met Long Wolf's great grandson at Wounded Knee on the Pine Ridge Reservation, and also other members of his family. Recently, the remains of Long Wolf were disinterred and returned to North America.

**Short Bull** :- Said to have been the leader of the Ghost Dancers as a 'high priest. He was a Brule Sioux.

**Kicking Bear** :- An Ogallala Sioux. He acted as a Government scout during the Ghost Dance campaign.

*Kicking Bear.*

**Black Heart** :- Travelled with the Wild West for two years. During the Ghost Dance rising he incurred great personal danger in order to promote peace.

**Plenty Wolves** :- Better known to the Wild West audiences as Yankton Charlie, he also acted as a Government scout during the Ghost Dance campaign, and was renowned for his courage.

**Lone Bull, Scatter, Revenge** :- Leading warriors in the Ghost

Dance uprising, they travelled in England with the Wild West in 1892.

**Rocky Bear and Red Dog** :- Spoke in defence of Buffalo Bill and the Wild West. Complaints were levelled by the Bureau of Indian Affairs about treatment of the Indians in the show in 1892, after unqualified statements by an Indian named White Horse. United States Consuls in Germany visited the showgrounds and decided there was no case to answer. Some of the Indians did wish to return home, but not due to bad treatment. Cody and Salsbury decided to disband and return home to face their critics, and it was then that Rocky Bear and Red Dog supported Cody and the show.

On the whole, treatment of the Indians within the show was at least as good as the other performers. Perhaps the worst of the experience was the crossing of the Atlantic, where many suffered from sea-sickness, and indeed some did die. Although we can marvel at the courage needed for such people to undergo the ordeal, life on the reservations was not particularly good for those used to the freedom of the plains, and the chance to travel, earn money and relive exciting times must have had appeal.

Other Indians with the Wild West over the years included:-

**Sitting Bull** (Tatanka Iyotake):- Toured with the Wild West for one season in Canada and the United States. He was brought from the Standing Rock reservation to join the show and had with him Indian Agent McLaughlin, a Scot, and two interpreters, William Halsey and Joseph Primeau. Mclaughlin's name would rise again later, as one of those who successfully rescinded Cody's mission to see Sitting Bull during the Ghost Dance uprising.

Upon joining the Wild West, Sitting Bull was fifty-one. With a deep voice, he was five feet eight inches tall, with a large head and broad shoulders, a tapering waist and small feet. He carried the facial scars of a smallpox epidemic in his youth. He was said to have killed his first buffalo when only ten years old. His pay with the show amounted to fifty dollars per week and a franchise

to sell his own autograph and postcards. Unable to comprehend that the rich white nation could allow beggars on the streets, he gave most of his money away to street urchins and boot-blacks. According to some accounts, Buffalo Bill gave Sitting Bull a trained, white horse as a gift on leaving the show. When the shots rang out that killed the Sioux, the horse automatically went into the routine that it had learned in the Wild West arena. After his death, Cody bought Sitting Bull's horse and returned him to performing in the arena, ridden by the bearer of the Stars and Stripes in the parade. Cody also bought Sitting Bull's cabin and re-erected it at the Colombian Exposition in Chicago in 1893. Beside it was the 'Ghost Pole', and two squaws selling souvenirs.

**Iron Tail** (Sinte Maza) :- With the Wild West for some years as the leading chief of the Indians, until the end of the show in 1913.

*Indian Maiden 'Shooting Star'.*

*Indians with the Wild West.*

*Indian with the Wild West.*

100

Whirlwind horse (Tasuke-wa-mini-ya-mini)
Joe Black Fox (Srigi-la-sapa)    Sam Lone Bear (Mato-wajila)
Flying Hawk (Ceata-ki-ya)    Little Elk (Wapli-ci-qa-la)

Black Fox; Iron-White-Man; Kills-Close-to-the-Lodge; American Horse (Samuel); Red-Horn-Bull; Amos -Two-Bulls; Black Elk; He Crow; Shooting Pieces; Tommy-Come-Last (child); Johnny Burke No-Neck child found on the field at Wounded Knee); Holy Bear; Paul Eagle Star; Bull-Stands-Behind; Flat Iron; Flies Above.

There were also Plenty Horses who carried five bullets in his body from Wounded Knee, and the Pawnee Chief, White Eagle, who was with the Wild West in 1885. Tribes featured in the show included Sioux (Brule, Hunkpapa, Ogallala), Cheyenne, Arapahoe, Wichitas and Pawnee.

Among the other performers with the Wild West were friends and acquaintances, many of who were from Cody's early life on the frontier.

**Buck Taylor** (King of the Cowboys)

Born in Fredericksburgh, Gillespie County, Texas in 1857, Taylor's real name was William Levi Taylor. His family had lived in Taos, Texas when the state had been still annexed to Mexico, and one of his uncles and grandfather had fought and perished at the Alamo. After the fight for Texas, only two male members of the family were left, Taylor's father and a younger brother. His father joined the Texas Cavalry at the outbreak of the Civil War and was killed in one of the first engagements. Upon the death of his mother, the eight year old William went to live with his uncle, who was a rancher, and it was here he learned the life of the cowboy. Growing to a height of well over six feet, his skills with horses and the lariat eventually led to him being made 'outfit boss', and he took part in many cattle drives over well known trails. After taking part in one such drive to Nebraska, he became known to Cody and his friend, Major North, eventually working for them on their ranch on the Dismal River.

*Indians with the Wild West. A postcard sold on the showgrounds during the tour of France.*

**Buffalo Bill's Wild West**

29. — Musiciens Peaux-Rouges

With the setting up of the Wild West, he was naturally offered a job, and quickly achieved star billing, leading the group of cowboys. Despite his size, Taylor was a most amiable and mild mannered individual, and like Cody, became a hero of the dime novel. First written by Prentiss Ingram, the first of these comic books was published in 1887 and the last in 1891. It is to Buck Taylor that we owe the standard image of the wandering cowboy hero that has endured to the present day.

Around 1892, Taylor left the Wild West to try to start his own show. Grateful to Cody, he parted with the Wild West on good terms.

## Johnny Baker (The Cowboy Kid)

Baker was born at O'Fallon's Bluffs on the South Platte River, Nebraska in 1870. His father Lew Baker was the owner of O'Fallon's Bluff Ranch, once an important landmark for the many cattle drives, and the overland Trail, which passed that way. Like Buck Taylor, Baker had grown up knowing cattlemen and their ways. With the decline of the cattle markets, Lew Baker moved to the town of North Platte where the railway was giving a boost to local economic growth. Here he built a large house. The house became a haven for 'old timers', who enjoyed telling stories of the old days and making free with Baker's hospitality. Eventually, the money ran out and the young Johnny had to find a sequence of jobs to support his father. This included working for Cody for a period. Cody took the young man under his wing and he soon became known as 'Buffalo Bill's boy', attending school in the winter months, where he attained a reasonable education. Having joined Cody in the Wild West, he sometimes acted as his assistant in the 'shooting from the saddle' act. He was also given shooting lessons by Annie Oakley.

Baker later became Scenic Director but after the close and eventual auction of the Wild West, Baker was asked by Cody to look after his affairs at his Camp Benito Mine. Baker eventually joined the Miller Brother's 101 Wild West and with it, returned to England once more. He had remained with Buffalo Bill's

*Johnny Baker.*

Wild West for its entire existence and after the death of Cody in 1917, later travelled in America giving lectures on his hero, and established a museum on Lookout Mountain, next to Buffalo Bill's grave.

**John Nelson** (Cha-sha-sha-na-po-ge-o) (Red Willow Fill the Pipe)

In the early days on the frontier, both white men and red had noted Nelson for his integrity. In his early life as a trapper and scout, he had guided Brigham Young and his Mormons across the desert to Utah. He Married the grand-daughter of the Ogallala Chief, Lone Wolf, and they had six children, all of whom appeared in the Wild West. Many photographs show nelson taking part in the 'Attack on a Settler's Cabin', and he occasionally took the reins of the Deadwood Stagecoach. He had appeared earlier with Cody on the stage, during the latter's thespian days. When James Bailey became involved with the Wild West and forced the introduction of side-shows, Nelson's family became a significant attraction on the midway.

**Tony Esquival** (Champion Vaquero Rider)

Esquival was born in Mexico, a descendant of Castillian ancestry, who had ranched along the Rio Grande. In his time he had been a Pony Express rider, cowboy and champion horseman. The chapter on the Wild West's visit to England in 1887/8 details the race between English thoroughbreds and range ponies, ridden by Esquival.

**'Major' John Burke** (Arizona John)

Of all those connected with the Wild West, Burke is possibly one of the most interesting, not for his rip-roaring achievements on the frontier but for his geniality, ability and tenacity. He was one of the few who remained with the show for the duration of its life. It is perhaps due to him that the visual images of the show have endured, not least for his florid testimonials in the programmes and intensive advertising arrangements.

Born in New York in the 'forties', Burke was the General Manager of the Wild West. Orphaned at two years old after the death of his father (and mother ten months before), he was given a home by relatives in Maryland, until the end of the Civil War. The Wild West programme states that after peace was declared

the young man, stimulated by stories of the frontier, joined General Green Clay Smith on an expedition to Montana. The General had been appointed Governor of Montana, then largely unknown territory, and the expedition was to establish him there. At that time, Nebraska City was the jumping off point for those travelling west, and it was here that Burke met Cody, and Major Frank North. The outbreak of the war with the Sioux impeded the progress of the expedition, but the journey gave the young Burke a view of the Indians and the frontier, which would

*Major John M. Burke.*

inflame his imagination. There may have been some exaggeration in this story for the benefit of the programme. Earlier in his career, in 1869, he had been a drama critic for a Washington newspaper. He let his hair grow, sometimes held back by pins, and gave himself the title of 'Arizona John'. His first meeting with Cody had been when Buffalo Bill was 'acting' in 'Scouts of the Prairie', Burke being the manager of the leading lady. It was thanks mainly to Burke's persuasive talents that Sitting Bull joined the Wild West for a season. Although to some extent self-invented - he also gave himself the prefix of 'Major' - there was little doubt that Burke did have considerable knowledge of Indian affairs and the military, claiming friends on both sides. His devotion to Buffalo Bill was genuine and the programmes bear witness in their enthusiastic text. Honest, sincere and generous, he was admirably fitted for his post as General Manager. In his dual role as press agent, he was at the time the highest salaried executive in the business.

*Princess Nouma-Hawa. A dwarf lady with Buffalo Bill's Wild West. The reverse of this post card confirms that she was also with Barnum & Bailey's Circus (Dated June 1904).*

## Lilian Smith (The California Girl)

Lillian was born at Coleville, Mono County, California, in the Autumn of 1871. At a time when importance was given to riding and shooting, it was still something of a novelty for a girl to be so proficient in both. At nine years old, she had been given a Ballard rifle (.22 calibre, and weighing seven pounds), and by July 1881 she was giving demonstrations at the Woodward Gardens in San Francisco. In 1883 she consolidated her reputation at a turkey shoot at Hollister, San Benito County, where at a distance of 150 yards she killed so many birds that her distance was increased to 200 yards. Still deadly accurate, she was asked to withdraw to give others a chance. Lillian joined the Wild West in 1886.

## Con Groner

Groner was the classical westerner. As the Sheriff of Lincoln County, Nebraska, he had once chased Jesse James over the state line and also crossed swords with the infamous 'Doc' Middleton gang. Ironically, in later years when Groner took part in the Wild West, Doc Middleton was also a performer and in 1886/7 the two lived side by side.

## Annie Oakley (Wan-tan-yeya-ci-sci-la) (Little Sure Shot . . . her Indian name, given by Sitting Bull, who considered her his adopted daughter.)

Woodland, Dark County was Annie's birthplace. She was born on 13th August, 1866. Like Lillian Smith, she was used to firearms from an early age and at fourteen had paid off her father's homestead mortgage with money she earned from the sale of game and skins. Annie's real name was Phoebe Anne Moses but almost from their first meeting, she was called 'Little Missy' by Buffalo Bill. She was a person of slight build, five feet tall and weighing only ninety eight pounds, and her name has become eternally linked with Buffalo Bill due to her success with the show. Her costume, while performing, consisting of a broad hat with uprolled brim, pleated skirt and leggings, has become an icon almost as marked as Cody himself.

December 16th, 1884, was the opening date for the 'World's Industrial & Cotton Exposition' in New Orleans, and Annie was at the time travelling with the Sells Brothers Circus which had a site opposite the Wild West. It was here that she first met Buffalo Bill and Co., and the rest is history. At one shooting match her opponent was another sharpshooter named Frank Butler. The outcome of the competition was that Annie walked away with the prize money but Butler walked off with Annie's heart, and shortly after the two were married. Butler became Annie's manager, all but giving up his own career.

Although there is a little controversy, she probably first met Sitting Bull around 1885. The Sioux was amazed by her trick shooting and made her his adopted daughter. It was due solely to the promise made by Major Burke to Sitting Bull that the latter

would see Annie Oakley every day, that he was persuaded to join the Wild West. In England in 1888, Annie quarrelled with Cody and she left the show, but later at Nate Salsbury's request, things were patched up and she returned, remaining with the show until 1901. In 1903, she took part in a shooting match at Blue River Park, Kansas City. It was the 'Grand American Handicap', and also taking part was a vaudeville performer with the name of 'Wenoma'. Wenoma's real name was Lillian Smith.

The Butler - Oakleys moved through a series of financially sound projects, joining the staff of the Carolina Hotel, Pinehurst, in 1915, where they took charge of the skeet range and gave lessons to guests. Among these were John D. Rockerfeller and John Philip Sousa, whose music featured so well in the Wild West. Annie wore tweeds and a feathered hat. When America joined the First World War, Annie and Frank Butler toured US Army camps giving demonstrations and encouragement to the troops.

**Nate Salsbury** (Wah-see-sha-e-ton-sha), ('Little White Chief' . . . his name given by Sitting Bull)

Along with Buffalo Bill, Salsbury must stand as the greatest influence on the Wild West. While Cody's head could at times be filled with the dash and dare of his own exploits, expanded into legend in the arena, Nate Salsbury was the main steadying and business force within the show. His double-entry book keeping maintained order within the finances of the Wild West, through good times and bad. He was born at Freeport, Illinois, on 28th February, 1846, and as the programme states, was a descendant of early Vermont settlers who fought in the War of Independence. Salsbury was said to have been the youngest enlisted man in the Army of the Cumberland during the Civil War, was wounded three times and ended the conflict in the Confederate prison at Andersonville. By 1888 he had found a vocation as an actor and travelled widely in America, India, Europe and Australia. He doubled also as stage manager and director. Always dressed formally with striped trousers, dark, tailed coat and derby hat, Salsbury married Rachel Samuels, the English soprano.

*A souvenir postcard which commemorates the Wild West's visit to England in 1903.*

## Others:-

There were many performers with the Wild West over the years, and gone but not quite forgotten yet, it is impossible to give full information on all. They included such men as 'Bridle Bill', who rode the infamous mule 'Suicide', twice daily, rain or shine. 'Mustang Jack' was called 'Pets-ze-ca-we-cha-' by the Indians and could catch the mane of a galloping horse and jump on its back. There was also 'Bronco Bill' Irving who still carried several bullets in his body from frontier incidents; Jim Mitchell was a champion roper; Jim Kidd, all round cowboy and Bill Bullock, who was half Sioux and half white; Captain Fred Matthews, who drove the Deadwood Stagecoach both in real life and in the show; 'Bronco John' and his performing black bear; Major Frank North, real hero of the frontier and former commander of Pawnee scouts; Captain Bogardus and his sons, (Bogardus was the inventor of the spring trap which ejected glass balls and clay pigeons to simulate the flight of birds). Then there were Frank Hammett, who was a champion bronc rider, John Highby, 'Coyote Bill', Seth Clover (Winchester sharpshooter) and Voter Hall, a Negro cowboy who rode an elk.

# WILL NEVER RETURN. . .

## 1903 / 4

*The final tour of the United Kingdom, including Yorkshire and Lincolnshire. Bad weather in Bradford. The aerial cyclist an accident. Good times and bad.*

Returning to London's Earle's Court, the Wild West began its final European tour on 26th December, 1902, Boxing Day. Again, Royalty paid its respects to Buffalo Bill when King Edward VII and Queen Alexandra visited the show in March 1903, together with the Princes, Edward and Albert.

Nate Slasbury's faltering health meant that he had been steadily unable to fulfil his managerial duties and James A. Bailey (of Barnum & Bailey's 'Greatest Show on Earth'), agreed a deal with Cody in that, for a share of all profits, he would provide local and transport expenses. The partnership had begun in April 1895, and when the 'Greatest Show on Earth' was touring Europe in 1898/9, the Wild West used Barnum and Bailey trains and rolling stock in the United States. Buffalo Bill would do this again in his final tour of Europe, using railway vehicles which the circus had specially built at Stoke-on-Trent, England. This was mutually beneficial for both shows as during these periods they were not in direct competition with each other.

The opening at Earle's Court was darkened by news of Salsbury's death at his home near Long Branch, New Jersey, on Christmas Eve. Flags on the showground flew at half mast and the colours carried in the arena by contingents of horsemen were fringed in black. Nate Salsbury would be sorely missed in the years to come.

The London engagement continued until 4th April, when the show moved on to Manchester's Brook's Bar. It then travelled to Liverpool, playing at the Old Exhibition Ground, Edge Lane estate, from 5th April to 23rd May, 1903. After London, some of the Indians who were there by special act of Congress, returned home.

Moving through one-day stands at Warrington and Birkenhead, the Wild West then turned south, into Wales, until returning on 1st June to play Birmingham until 13th. The show was erected at Aston Lane, Perry Bar, and did quite well, apart from one occasion when the performance clashed with a football match played by Aston Villa.

A meandering path of short stands continued back into Wales, the Midlands, the south of England and the West Country. This was not haphazard, however, but calculated so as not to play any one area for too long. When returning to a locality, there were sure to be those who had not yet seen the show, and prompted by newspapers and word of mouth, would make the effort to swell the grandstands.

By August the show was in Kent but moving back north, through Canterbury, Colchester, Norwich, Leicester and finally entering Lincolnshire at Spalding on 22nd September, 1903. The bill poster for the Holbeach area, Bill Quires, spent the previous week in preparation to advertise the coming of the Wild West.

### Spalding (Wednesday 23rd September, 1903)

Leaving Leicester at around midnight, the three special trains arrived at Spalding via Saxby and Bourne in the early morning. At Cunningham's Drove the engines were uncoupled, to change ends in order to bring the trains into the station in a manner ready for eventual departure. Around Stepping Stone Lane, many who had risen early to witness the de-training gathered. The usual slick operation was carried out to the admiration of the onlookers, and road vehicles began to trail toward the field owned by Mr. Green Waltham. This area, also known as Green Waltham's Park and situated on the Pinchbeck Road, was found to be soft under foot, wagons having to be double teamed to overcome the problem. The canvas city was erected within three hours, and already the crowds were beginning to inspect the grounds, still some time before the performance began. Being particularly fascinated by the Indians, reports note two Sioux babies born at Spalding. The side show initiated by James Bailey also did a brisk trade with its magicians, snake charmers, sword swallowers and the dog-faced man. On the grounds, all manner of souvenirs could be purchased, such as Cody's life story, (written by himself), and copies of the 'Rough Rider', a journal of the Wild West show published by Cody and Salsbury.

Buffalo Bill was now fifty-seven, but the Spalding Free Press described him as a fine, 'picturesque figure riding his horse like a centaur'. The two shows, at two o' clock in the afternoon and eight in the evening, were packed, over fourteen thousand attending each performance. As Buffalo Bill introduced the 'Congress of Rough riders', he stressed that the Wild West was not a circus, but a truly realistic exhibition, the participants merely re-enacting the roles that they had worn in real life. In his own act, Cody was accompanied by Johnny Baker, who tossed glass balls into the air for Buffalo Bill to shoot down. Baker was also remembered in Spalding for his own feats of marksmanship, when it was noted that he used a rifle with a magazine. Cody entered the arena again later, dressed as 'Teddy' Roosevelt, for the 'Attack on San Juan Hill', a re-enactment of an incident during the recent Spanish-American War. Also taking part were detachments of the 9th and 10th US Cavalry, Grime's Battery and Garcia's Cuban Scouts, with Indians playing the part of Spanish troops.

After the evening show, the side-show remained open for a while, but many of the other canvas buildings were already being taken down and packed onto the road vehicles, which would then be loaded on the trains which would take the Wild West on to Boston.

## Boston (Thursday 24th September, 1903)

In the early light, the great Wild West rumbled into Boston and was met with the usual throng of early risers, determined not to miss one detail of the show while it was in their town. Unlike the 'Greatest Show on Earth', which had previously visited the area, Buffalo Bill encouraged this kind of interest in his show. It created a kind of audience participation in the events. Visitors who wandered freely through the showgrounds would spread goodwill by word of mouth. Barnum & Bailey had always ensured that the menagerie was unloaded first and reloaded first, to minimise any 'free viewing' by the public.

The site of the Wild West event was Ryan's Field, on the Sleaford Road, which the Boston Guardian and Lincolnshire Independent reported 'had not seen so much traffic since Barnum & Bailey's 'Greatest Show on Earth' was with us in 1898'. The reporter described the initial rendering of the 'Star Spangled Banner' by the cowboy band as 'a blare of an unusual kind of music', but the grand entry as one of the finest of spectacular effects. He noted the individual groups of riders, introduced with a fanfare and drum accompaniment, going on to say. . . 'First and foremost came the picturesque Indians, and then followed in turn the wild looking Cossacks; the South American Gauchos; the wiry Mexicans; the daring cowboys; Roosevelt's Rough Riders; United States Cavalrymen with the Stars and Stripes floating in the wind; British Cavalry, one of whom bore triumphantly aloft, the Union Jack of my native land for the honour of which, whatever the merits or demerits of the struggle, these men and thousands of others fought in the South African War'. The crowds roared equally as they beheld both British and American flags alike.

As the afternoon performance ended, the crowds leaving for home met the fringes of another coming early for the evening show. Those who attended in the evening were given the benefit of added atmosphere created by the electric lighting. Once ended, the rumbling wagons could be heard again down the Sleaford Road, as the Wild West dismantled and returned to the station.

## Grantham (Friday 25th September, 1903)

As usual, the detraining was flawless in the early dawn light as the canvas was again erected. This day the showground was on a large field close to the barracks which had formerly been used as a drill ground by 4th Battalion, the Lincolnshire Regiment. Local hostelries did good business that day, in the manner of a normal Saturday, but no weekend had ever been like this before, with Cossacks and Indians strolling around the thoroughfares of Grantham. Of course this caused much interest and was good publicity for the Wild West and Buffalo Bill.

The area was the headquarters for the Belvoir Hunt, and many drawn from this activity were present in the audience to appreciate the many fine feats of horsemanship by the 'Rough Riders of the World'. Many Englishmen admired the McClellan saddles of the American cavalry. Designed by the Civil War General of that name, who served with the Northern Army, these saddles had a light skeleton with an open centre, and had also impressed General Gateacre of the British Army, who visited the show at Colchester.

The riding of the bucking broncos attained much admiration and each section was universally accepted as being 'totally genuine'. Although the shooting by Johnny Baker was again marvelled at in Grantham, many thought Buffalo Bill far superior, in that he fired from the saddle of a galloping horse. The fact that he occasionally missed did not detract.

Because of the fear of Foot and Mouth disease, prevalent at the time, the buffalo herd was not allowed to enter the country during this period, and therefore this item was deleted from the list of events, and not included in the publicity.

**Lincoln (Saturday 26th September, 1903))**

The high, bright posters again heralded the coming of the Wild West, this time to the City of Lincoln. They exaggerated the three special trains into 'four', and told of the forthcoming 'living object lesson' given by the 'mounted warriors of the world'; 'a gathering of extraordinary consequence to fittingly depict all that virile, muscular manhood has and can endure'.

The venue was the Racecourse and tickets were available from Harston & Son, the Pianoforte and Organ purveyors of 228, High Street. A free entertainment was announced for visitors to the grounds at eleven o' clock by the 'famous Cowboy Military Band'. Surprisingly, the attendance for both shows was rather poor, with eight thousand in the afternoon and only slightly more for the evening presentation.

A reporter for the Lincolnshire Echo interviewed Cody in his personal railway car and was pleasantly surprised at the vehicle, fitted out with bathroom, sleeping quarters, office and living accommodation. As always Buffalo Bill was most hospitable, knowing well by now the importance of good publicity. The reporter was charmed by Cody in both his appearance and manner, noting in a later article that the great scout did not look his age. He also noticed the Masonic Order of the 32nd Degree, which Buffalo Bill wore on his chest, given him at South Brookland. He also wore an exquisite scarf pin, presented to him a short time before, by King Edward VII, and a heavy gold chain and horseshoe with nine diamonds for nails.

The weather was generally fine and despite the somewhat disappointing crowds, the shows went well. Prices were as usual, one, two, three and four shillings, with box seats at five shillings and seven shillings and sixpence. Except for the shilling seats, children were admitted at half price, but no seats under four shillings could be booked in advance. Tickets at all prices were also available on the showground during times of opening. Patrons were also delighted by the American and other accents of the attendants who showed them to their places.

Between the hours of midnight and two in the morning, the three trains left Lincoln, arriving at the next stand by five o' clock in the morning.

**Leeds (Monday 28th September to 3rd October, 1903)**

Buffalo Bill's Wild West next visited Leeds, rolling into town during the early hours of Sunday 27th September, on the Great Northern Railway. It was the custom that Sunday was always maintained as a rest day, with no performances given. So after the essential canvas was erected, around ten o' clock, the staff and performers were free to pursue their own recreations. As some of the show people meandered toward the city centre, where as always they were the centre of attention, the trams

*Beaded scabbard belonging to Sam Bear and Tom Payne's cuffs.*

*The Broken whip dropped during the street parade in Leeds.*

going in the opposite direction, towards Kirkstall, were beginning to fill with sightseers. The jewellers and other tradesmen of central Leeds did a brisk trade during the time of the Wild West, in sales of cheap trinkets, beads and other minor items, mainly to the Indians.

The show site was the Cardigan Fields, an area of common land already being reduced in size due to commercial pressure. It was at this time still large enough to house a show the size of the Wild West. This was the second time that the show had been seen on Cardigan Fields, occupying the same site on its visit in 1891.

Unlike many previous stands, the stay in Leeds was to last a week. The first afternoon performance was fully booked, and many were turned away. Lone Bear led the detachment of Indian warriors as they sped, bareback, down the length of the arena, resplendent in feathers and paint. When all of the riders were drawn up, Buffalo Bill entered on a big, black horse, the latter

*Edward Whitworth and sister. Edward can be seen holding the whipstock retrieved by his father.*

110

wearing the silver-mounted bridle presented to Cody by the King, when he had been the Prince of Wales. If any part of the show was appreciated more, it was probably the large set-piece re-enactments, more enthusiastically reported by the pressmen. Again, the attack on San Juan Hill was very well received, as was the pursuit of the Deadwood coach by Indians. By this time, the original had long since seen better days, and had been presented to the Smithsonian Institute in Washington. Another was specially commissioned, to be saved by 'scouts and cowboys', to the accompaniment of Mr. Sweeney's cowboy band and J.P. Sousa.

On the morning of Thursday 1st October, a street parade left the showground at ten o' clock. At the head of the column was Buffalo Bill, leading a most colourful array of brightly dressed horsemen, wagons, horses and even the mobile electric lighting plant, to the accompaniment again of the cowboy band. Cody rode in a four wheel carriage with hickory wheels, drawn by two beautiful greys, for once discarding his buckskins for a more formal frock coat. The parade wound around Kirkstall Road, St. Matthias Road, Burley Road, Hyde Park Road, Woodhouse Lane, Cookridge Street, Park Row and the City Square, Wellington Street and back along Kirkstall Road to Cardigan Fields. Among the crowds watching the parade around Briggate was a small boy, Edward Whitworth, with his father. As the line of horsemen passed by, a horse shied and reared for some reason and the wrist loop of the rider's whip broke, releasing the handle which fell to the ground. Leaving the broken whip, the procession moved on and Edward's father dashed out from the pavement, gathering up the handle, like the story of the show, to be passed down through further generations of the family. A photograph was taken shortly after of the young Edward, with the whip stock that had once belonged to Buffalo Bill's Wild West.

That week at the Coliseum, Hercat the well known magician and ventriloquist was, to some extent, drawing audiences away from the western show. Producing money by 'magic', he was assisted by Miss Florrie Fairfax, vocalist and mimic.

## Bradford (October 5th and 6th, 1903)

Moving on to Bradford, the show was erected at a site on the Leeds Road, Thornbury, which was previously used by Barnum & Bailey. Large crowds gathered at the opening performance that Monday, despite the weather being very wet, chilly and unsettled. As the wind increased, additional precautions were made to secure the canvas, much of it being double pegged. Performances were at the normal times of two o' clock and eight o' clock, with tickets available from Wood and Marshall's music warehouse at 9, Ivegate. Doors to the showground would open an hour prior to the performance time, with one ticket admitting the holder to all advertised attractions.

Leeds Road became a promenade for show people of all kinds, followed by knots of locals, who would undoubtedly never see anything like it again. Some of the show folk wandered into town, or visited the trains, where their belongings were stored. White Cloud was photographed by a local newspaper outside his teepee, but as photographs only became more commonplace in the press around 1909, the picture was never published and probably no longer exists.

Notes were taken by reporters of the prodigious appetites of the Indians. . .

". . . The Red Man is very comfortable in camp, and he is very well fed. He dines at one corner of the great tent, somewhat apart from the hundreds of artists and helpers, and his appetite is amazing. His first course at luncheon consisted of four boiled eggs and a dish of stew served at the same time. This was his modest beginning. There was much roast pork and vegetables to follow. The Sioux take kindly to pig."

It was discovered that Hassan, the Persian giant from the side-show, was the smallest eater in camp, and that most of the cowboys had long since lost the incentive to 'hoorah' every town that they visited.

*Buckskin Jacket which once belonged to a Wild West performer. Buffalo Bill?*

Some surprise was shown by pressmen that the catering staff included a Frenchman, an Italian and an Irishman, along with the Americans.

Tuesday's afternoon performance in Bradford, attended by the Mayor, was given through a downpour of incessant rain, and boards and tons of straw were laid to enable the public to reach their seats with dry feet. The big arena, 414 feet long by 180 feet wide, had become a quagmire and horses struggled through the exhibition with mud up to their knees. As the rain subsided, the wind increased in severity, and despite an assurance by the management, the evening show had to be cancelled in the interests of public safety. This would have been the 307th consecutive performance. Cody made an announcement in which he thanked the people of Bradford for their support and apologised for being unable to make the last presentation. Strangely, when the 'Greatest Show on Earth' had visited Bradford in 1899, the evening performance on the second day had also been abandoned due to high winds.

### Keighley (October 7th, 1903)

*Keighley town centre 1903 showing (bottom left) a large poster(s) advertising the visit of the Wild West.*

The rain continued as the Wild West arrived at Keighley. Leaving the trains that Wednesday morning, the wagons rolled up Cavendish Street, rounding the Mechanics' Institute into Skipton Road, Utley, where again a site used by Barnum & Bailey was utilised. As the canvas was struck, the weather cleared and by noon the sun was shining. Rumours of a free morning show were circulating but this was possibly a misunderstanding of the pre-show entertainments. Never the less, several hundred people made their way very early up the Skipton Road.

The afternoon show had seven thousand attending and in the evening, ten thousand.

Prior advertising had been carried out some time before and in the centre of town, a large 24 sheet poster appeared on hoardings surrounding the Corporation dump. It showed Buffalo Bill in one pose, seated upon a white horse, and another of him at the head of a column of banner carrying cavalrymen. Other views on the poster depicted a portrait of Cody facing an Indian Chief and squadrons of mounted riders. The site is now the Town Hall Square.

Archibald Ramsden's Piano Saloon of 7, North Street, was the place in Keighley where tickets to the Wild West were obtainable, or at the showground, and it was mainly the lower priced seats that were taken by the general public. As always, special excursions brought people from many miles away, and in Keighley itself, six Corporation trams were continuously kept busy ferrying patrons to the show. A record number of passengers was carried by the trams that day, beating the previous one for Barnum & Bailey's Circus in 1899, but even so, this proved not enough and enterprising carriage owners made the most of the Wild West being in town.

Tributes were paid locally to the show, both in its execution and organisation. Although military aspects were applauded, especially sabre drill by the 10th US Negro Cavalry and tent-pegging by English Lancers, the drill by a crew of the US Life Saving Corps was also appreciated, probably due to its novelty.

As early as four o' clock, some of the tents not needed were struck and carried back to the waiting trains at the Keighley Midland Railway goods station. Following the evening show, as the rest of the ground was dismantled, crowds watched the retreating Wild West as a performance in its own right. Opposite the Utley Weslyan Chapel a man fell beneath the wheels of an omnibus, but luckily his injuries proved minor. One youngster who had missed the show was Arthur Pakes, a butcher's boy, who on crossing Cavendish Street, was hailed by someone in a four wheel carriage, drawn by two greys. Looking up into the bespectacled eyes of Buffalo Bill he was asked for directions to the Queens Theatre. Walter Melville's Company was presenting 'Her Second Time on Earth', and arriving some way through, the play was paused while a standing ovation was given to Cody.

### Halifax (October 8th 1903)

The first train pulled into Pellon Station at three-thirty in the morning and began to disembark for another one day stand at Halifax. Before many were awake, most of the canvas city had been raised.

Again, poor weather prevailed, but the management were determined that no more performances would be cancelled and with all usual enthusiasm, played to good audiences at Savile Park, known also as the Moor. A mist which settled on the field for the evening show gave an eerie feel to the events and even the big spotlights had difficulty in adding to the illumination of the arena, but some thought that this added to the atmosphere and authenticity.

Considerable interest was shown in the coming of the Wild West by local inhabitants of the area. A week before, Major Burke had visited the town to ensure all arrangements were in order, and settled the forty pounds asked for by the Corporation for the rent of the ground. Burke reassured many who doubted that the show would come to Halifax, explaining that the Wild West was organised in the manner of an army, each man and horse knowing their place and duties. He confirmed that the show would be exactly the same as that given in London before members of the Royal Family.

A reporter for the Halifax Evening Courier managed to secure an interview with Buffalo Bill. Apart from being impressed with the man himself, the reporter expressed amazement that Cody never seemed to catch cold, despite being dogged by inclement weather.

While tickets could be obtained from W. Hemingway's Piano and Organ Warehouse at 11, Northgate, they were again available on the showground, where a preliminary open air concert was given by the cowboy band at eleven that morning.

## Wakefield (October 9th, 1903)

Surprisingly little was reported on the Wild West's one day stand at Wakefield. All that seems to have survived of the visit is the standard newspaper advertisement in the Wakefield Express on 3rd October heralding the coming event, for some reason the town's press giving little attention to such a huge entertainment. All that we do know to date is that the site of the event was the Belle Vue Grounds and that J. Dunnill's Pianoforte Warehouse was the place where tickets could be obtained other than the showground.

## Doncaster (October 10th, 1903)

The Town Moor in Doncaster was to be the next venue of the Wild West. Potential audiences were assured by the press that for 'one bob' (one shilling) patrons would see just as much as a box seat holder, and that as tickets were numbered and dated they were restricted to the seating capacity.

Cody and his staff were much satisfied with business at Doncaster. Apart from a few of the higher priced seats, the stands were virtually full, meaning that well over 20,000 people visited the show. Bearing in mind the continuous side-show entertainment and the souvenir trade, takings must have been excellent. Some of the newspaper reports suggest a lack of variety in the programme, perhaps missing the point that the Wild West was not a circus but an American Exhibition which expanded the equestrian theme with other riders from around the world. The lighting arrangements at the evening performance were also criticised, indicating that some parts of the arena were not as well lit as others, but remind us that moveable spotlights followed the principal participants.

Due to the poor weather conditions, access to the showground across the Race Common proved treacherous, deep ruts made by wagons and omnibuses causing problems for pedestrians, especially after dark.

After the evening performance the three sections of the entrained Wild West moved out at midnight, one o' clock and two o' clock, bound for Sheffield.

## Sheffield (12 - 15th Ocober, 1903)

The Midland Railway Company was responsible for conveying the Wild West into the City of Sheffield, the engines bringing the show into the Queens Road goods shed early on the morning of the 12th.

Buffalo Bill remained in his private car, dealing with correspondence that morning while the show was being erected, and was once again cornered by a reporter, this time from the Sheffield Daily Telegraph. Ever conscious of the need for good publicity, the showman granted an audience and, pressed by the newspaperman by an account of his early life, Cody talked of his struggle with the sub-chief, Yellow Hand, shortly after the demise of Custer, in July 1876. He showed the reporter the knife which he had used to take the scalp of the Indian, the former showing some surprise at the words embossed into the bright steel. . .
. . . 'Made in Sheffield.'

Other reporters visited the grounds, there being no performances that Sunday, and as usual were most impressed by the hospitality shown them. Poor weather continued and most of the camp spent the day under canvas. Some newsmen spoke to the contingent of English Cavalrymen, some of whom had served with Baden Powell in South Africa. Another noticed one of Roosevelt's Rough Riders shaving a Cuban.

The site for the show in Sheffield was Thompson's Meadow, Penistone Road, Owlerton, where it had appeared twelve years earlier in 1891.

Buffalo Bill is said to have visited Richard Herringshaw, sexton of the Church at Owlerton, during this last visit to the area. The building was situated close to the showground and Mr. Herringshaw, being a very keen gardener, was only too pleased to spend time with Cody on several occasions, talking 'flowers'. This is not as unusual as it may seem, as previously Buffalo Bill had appeared at Earle's Court at the same time as an exhibition staged by the Agricultural Society.

From Sheffield the Wild West moved to Chesterfield for a short stand, then Nottingham, Loughborough, Derby and Burton, closing the season on 23rd October, 1903. Some of the cast returned home while others remained at the winter quarters near Stoke, provided by Renshaws, the engineering company who had been responsible for the manufacture of the railway rolling stock used by the show.

The 1904 season began at Stoke-on-Trent on the 25th April, with a one day stand at the Old Race Course, Boothen Farm, in that town. Lost for this year was the battle for San Juan Hill, to be replaced by a representation of the Battle of the Little Big Horn, or 'Custer's Last Stand'. This was possibly due to the fact that the show was travelling in a small country, and although different venues would be played, they would still be close to places previously visited. To encourage prior patrons to come again, the management had obviously made every effort to keep the entertainment fresh within the well known image of the Wild West. Also new were the ' Intrepid Cowboy Cyclist' and The Imperial Japanese Troupe, but many of the tried and tested events of previous years remained. The previous season had lasted 28 weeks and another was about to begin.

## Mansfield (27th June, 1904)

The Wild West moved south playing several stands in Wales, and leaving Cardiff on the 21st May, followed the rails to the West Country with one day visits to Exmouth, Torquay, Penzance, Cambourne, Truro, Bodmin, Plymouth and Taunton on the 4th June. Then east to skirt the capital, with stops at many places including Dorchester, Southampton, Windsor, Wimbledon and then to Cambridge on the 24th and Ilkeston on 25th June. Continuing north the show entered Mansfield on the morning of Sunday June 26th, 1903, and with the usual smooth execution made of the detraining, moved onto the showground at Westfield Lane. Pre-advertising had made much of the new attractions and as always, colourful posters had appeared all over the area some weeks before. In the Mansfield Reporter, an advertisement was taken beneath that of the show by the proprietors of the Oriental Café, West Gate, inviting all visitors to Mansfield 'on the occasion of Buffalo Bill's Wild West', to take their ease at their premises.

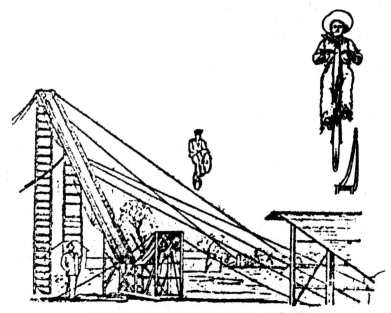

THE DARING BICYCLE FEAT.

*Carter the Cowboy cyclist.*

Around 19,000 were estimated to have attended the two performances of the show on Monday 27th June. Earlier, Frank Small, Cody's press bureau man, had escorted several parties of newspapermen around the grounds, explaining the various section tents and their functions and also scotching rumours that Buffalo Bill would not be present for the show. As always, they marvelled at the organisation and the clock-like regularity that was vital to the smooth running of the Wild West. Hundreds had attended the arrival and followed the wagons down to Westfield Lane, mixing with the Indians, Japanese and Cossacks. Previously, however, the local press had been instructed by Cody that no-one would be admitted during church hours on Sunday.

The afternoon performance was progressing well until it came time for Carter, the cowboy cyclist to present his act. Carter was in fact George C. Davis, an American, who as the programme described, descended 85 feet down an inclined ramp, and after gathering speed towards the bottom curve, was propelled by momentum across a gap of 41 feet to land upon another ramp which should have returned him to the ground safely. Unfortunately, the cyclist did not land squarely on this occasion and his handlebar collided with an arc lamp which had been placed too close to his intended path. As he lay motionless, Dr Nesbitt of Sutton-in-Ashfield, and Dr Oldham of Mansfield, who were present, rushed to his aid and helped to carry Davis to the rear of the arena. After regaining consciousness, the man was found to have only a slight concussion and minor abrasions to his head and face, and after having them bandaged, was taken by cab to the local hospital. Missing the evening performance, Davis was advised by doctors to remain at the hospital for a few days, but contrary to their advice, insisted on returning to the Wild West before it moved on to Rotherham.

## Rotherham (28th June, 1904)

Tuesday morning saw the three special trains rolling into Rotherham, with 49 cars weighing 1,184 tons, with a combined length of three quarters of a mile. The great western exhibition moved in the early morning down towards a field off Sheffield Road, Ickles, where it was viewed by early rising locals. The weather proved fine and warm, and the roustabouts once more raised the canvas ready for another show.

Those who wished to pre-book their seats could do so at the Rotherham Express in the town. Many took advantage of the concert given by Mr Sweeney's cowboy band or attended the side-show which opened three hours before the first performance. That evening the Wild West was honoured with the presence of Mr George Clarke, the Mayor, and his retinue. The cowboy cyclist was omitted from the programme, more due to his damaged machine than to his personal injuries.

Foreigners were hardly ever seen by the public, and the sight of so many at one time must have been quite a culture shock for British audiences. They admired the 10th Negro Cavalry and their sabre drill. Initially mustered during the Civil War, these horsemen were known as 'Buffalo Soldiers' by the Indians, who likened their tight curly hair to the heavy shoulder hide of the bison. It is interesting to note at this stage, that Russia and Japan were at war in the Far East and on many occasions, the press were prompted to ask how the Samurai and Cossack horsemen in the show got on together. Perhaps not surprisingly, no reports suggest any animosity between the two groups and indeed some go as far as describing them sitting at the same table for meals. Whether this was totally true or not, the Rotherham press prompted their readers to compare the merits of the performers in both stature and horsemanship only. There were generally around nineteen Cossacks in the show and twelve Japanese. The Japanese were under the leadership of Toro, who had 'served as sergeant in the army of the Mikado for nine years'.

By midnight, the field on Sheffield Road had been cleared. The Wild West moved on to the next stand, leaving only crumpled straw and hundreds of spent cartridges for the youngsters of the town to collect.

**Gainsborough (29th June, 1904))**

Mr. A. Butler, of the Marquis of Granby Hotel in Gainsborough was obviously a man of some enterprise and forethought, for beneath the advertisement for Buffalo Bill's Wild West in the local newspaper was another which read. . .

MARQUIS OF GRANBY HOTEL
WILL SUPPLY REFRESHMENTS
During the above visit in the field adjoining
FINEST ALES, SPIRITS, AERATED WATERS and
SANDWICHES etc.
Convenience will be made to cater for cyclists. Machines Stabled at twopence each and a numbered ticket given.

How well Mr. Butler did on this day is not recorded.

Highfield Farm was where the Wild West set up camp, with tickets available from B. Wealls, a stationer of Silver Street.

'Custer's Last Stand' was hailed as a 'triumph for the show' by Gainsborough Crowds, although as history dictates, it was more so for the Indians. We learn from the press at this time that although Sitting Bull had only been with the show for one season in the US and Canada, his son was one of the Sioux taking part there in the re-enactment. (The newspaper gives his name as William Sitting Bull).

Again note was taken of the 'friendly' rivalry between the Cossacks and the Samurai due to the hostilities of their countries. During this season, the two groups actually appeared, with others, in the same act.

Oropeza, the brilliant roper was cheered along with his Mexican companions. The cowboy cyclist was back in action, but now the Gainsborough press recorded his descent from one hundred feet. This is either a mistake or exaggeration as the ramp was in fact only eighty five feet long, and the actual angled height probably around forty feet.

At Gainsborough we are given another insight into activities outside the showground. Street parades were not always given but the side-show, and free concert given by the cowboy band always drew large crowds. It was not unusual, therefore, as we have already seen, for the enterprising to make the most of the visit by the Wild West.

Some, like the off-ground vendors, plied their trade honestly. However, the prices charged here could be exorbitant. Strawberries being offered to those approaching for the evening performance at sixpence, were reduced to three pence on the way home. This was apparently also the case with meat pies. Purveyors of all kinds encircled the showground with goods for sale, ranging from aerated waters to cheap jewellery and carted up on anything from horse-drawn wagons to perambulators. Beside the vendors, there were those of a more dubious nature. Pickpockets and those who would not, or could not, work, plying the crowds as beggars. The police drafted in men from other divisions to supervise the vast number of people and maintain a presence to dissuade felons. They were also needed near the ticket office where business was brisk, and some in fear of not obtaining a ticket of admission had been known to lose their self control.

## Grimsby (30th June, 1904)

Another tide of American fashion was spreading over England and the Wild West thundered into the imaginations of the people of Grimsby. De-training was by now virtually a part of the performance, and at two fifteen in the morning the first section, via the Great Central Railway, arrived at the West Marsh sidings, followed at thirty minute intervals by the other two. Dis-embarkation began at five, with the two hundred heavy draught horses being the first to leave the train by means of ramps. They were kept in harness during their time on the trains so once arrived at a new stand, they could be ready for work immediately. Their task once completed, they would have the rest of the day at ease. With no spoken word, each animal moved into exactly the right place, ready to be hitched to the wagons, which were then being unloaded from the flat cars. Those watching were always amazed at the precision, speed and lack of noise from such a mighty army of workers.

Just before six in the grey morning light, the first Indian appeared from one of the sleeping cars, wrapped in a blanket. During the next few minutes, he was followed by nearly three hundred Mexicans, Cossacks, cowboys, Cubans, and many others. Their mounts were de-trained by grooms and as each found his horse, they filed out of the goods yard, heading toward the Old Artillery Field, Clee Road, where the show was to be held. A route man was stationed at every corner to ensure a swift passage to the ground and it was four hours later when the last piece of equipment arrived. Breakfast had been ready in the cook tent by six-thirty and the teamsters took turns to eat. Teams of tent-peggers were already at work and men were shinning the poles to lay canvas when Buffalo Bill arrived in his carriage, personally taking charge of events. The show was likened to a portable town, each knowing his place and responsibilities and with specialist workers who could cope with any emergency.

As always, the reporters were in force, encouraged by the Wild West press department to watch the canvas evolve, and take breakfast with the show people. They sat shoulder to shoulder with Indians and cowboys, dining on steak and potatoes, strawberries and cream, presented by white-hatted cooks on snow-white, clean tablecloths. What a sight it must have been. Eating with the newsmen were Buffalo Bill, Jules Keen (his business manager), Starr (treasurer), and Frank Small. Small, a press agent for the Wild West, was a man of large proportions. Tanned and with grizzled hair, his appearance somewhat masked his courteousness and good humour, and before working for Cody, he had been a roving reporter for a large American newspaper. After leaving the dining tent, the reporters were astounded that the arena had already been erected, and never did they see men work as hard as they did that morning at the Wild West.

Those who obtained tickets, either from the ticket wagon or at Holder Brothers Piano Warehouse at 25, Victoria Street, had the experience of a lifetime for just a few pennies. For some, there was excitement even before the entertainment on the showground. Harry Dalby was seventeen in 1904, and well remembered in later years how he literally had to fight to obtain tickets in a disorderly crowd, coming away with a black eye for his perseverance.

The coming of the Wild West created a holiday atmosphere, and Mr. Patchett of the George Hotel in Caistor arranged to take a party to the show in his wagonette. To save the horses, passengers were required to walk out of town to the top of Top House Hill before alighting. Once at Grimsby, the animals were stabled at the Dolphin Hotel. Afterwards the party found a café ordering ham and eggs before returning home.

The day of the show corresponded with the opening ceremony of Grant-Thorold Park, next to the site where the Wild West was established. Cody had made the decision to include Grimsby in the tour the previous November, and despite learning of the conflicting event some weeks before, was unable to change his plans as other venues would be affected.

The park was a gift to the town by Mr. A.W.T. Grant-Thorold and the Grant-Thorold family. Flying bunting heralded the celebrations to come. Before noon that Thursday, a large marquee had been erected on one of the lawns and was to be used for a luncheon which would follow the initial opening. Although the weather was fine and sunny, the wind strengthened until at around eleven o' clock, part of the marquee blew down onto chairs and tables below, disrupting the preparations.

It was feared by the park staff that the rest of the structure was in imminent state of collapse. Help was soon at hand with the arrival of Fred Hutchinson, one of Buffalo Bill's managers, who with a company of Wild West canvas men, began to re-rig the marquee. At this stage, however, the officials decided not to take any risk in the high winds, and that luncheon would be taken in the open air. Within minutes, Cody's men had complied and had taken down the big tent and stored it away. The assistance of the Wild West was referred to in speeches, later that day.

Everything that the posters promised was there, arrayed before the awed crowds at the two performances in a swirl of colour and daring. Then those who cared to watched the wigwams and the side-show being dismantled. Those who stood at the corner of Park Street and Wellington Street (then not built up) in the area now known as Fiveways, saw the tops of the stands being taken down as the audience was leaving the last performance. By two in the morning, gone were the Cossacks, the Indians, and the Wild West, and all was quiet once more on the Old Artillery Field.

## Hull (1st & 2nd July, 1904)

In 1904, the fairground at Walton Street, as it is today, was a strange, desolate part of the city next to the West Park, but for two days in July that year, the atmosphere would be different. Buffalo Bill's Congress of Rough Riders would change all of that, and by seven in the morning of July 1st, the fairground was a bustle of activity. Teams of ten men surrounded large iron stakes which had to be pounded several feet into the ground with heavy jack-hammers. Each man brought down his hammer in a rhythm with his neighbour with such force and rapidity that the stake was hot to the touch. Some of the smaller stakes were made of wood with iron hoops to strengthen them.

Holder's Piano Warehouse (in Whitefriargate) would supply tickets and while no certain evidence has come to light, it has been suggested that a street parade took place, followed by a mock attack on a wagon train, taking place at the Boulevard, close to the showgrounds. There is either some confusion with the actual performance on the fairground or perhaps something put on by other (less impressive) western shows, which came some time later. Although street parades were very often given by the Wild West, rarely would anything more elaborate be staged, due to restrictions of traffic and time.

A Hull Daily Mail reporter visited the Wild West for the traditional press breakfast where, along with hot, strong coffee, the menu offered beefsteak, stewed tripe or liver and bacon with potatoes, cooked in the 'Irish fashion', followed by strawberries and cream. In the customary tour of the showgrounds the reporter noted the stable tents. As grooms were putting down fresh straw he examined the saddles used by the various groups of horsemen, which were hung over a cable running down the centre of the tent. Some were 'hard as granite' and 'exceedingly large', while others were of minute proportions'.

Some watching the performance found the Japanese not as skilled in the saddle as the Russians, but were popular, none the less. Light was fading at the evening performance when the two groups appeared and some friendly rivalry was seen between them. The good nature seen between the two groups at this time must have been somewhat uneasy as the papers carried vivid accounts of the war between their respective countries. Around this time, reports were coming through of Admiral Kamimara's confrontation with the Vladivostock Squadron near Iki Island. The Japanese warships opened fire upon the three Russian Cruisers returning from the bombardment of Gensan, and in the same period Admiral Togo led a successful torpedo raid on Port Arthur with the loss of one officer and thirty men. While elsewhere in the arena, Arab acrobats vied for the attention of the audience, most interesting to the crowds in Hull were the battle sequences such as 'Custer's Last Rally'. It may interest the reader to note that Custer's widow visited Hull in 1894, staying a week in the city.

The lasting impression of the show was the rapidity with which everything was carried out. As one act left the arena, the next was already entering, ensuring constant attention. Around fifty thousand were said to have attended during the two day visit of the Wild West.

A cartoonist in the Hull News on Saturday July 9th used the theme of the Wild West to show the plight of Mr. Balfour's government, with the Prime Minister dressed in cowboy attire, clinging to the back of a plunging mustang whose brand is marked as 'Office' and 'Elections'.

The caption reads. . .

"Mr. Balfour declares that the Government has no intention of resigning, and sees no reason for an early dissolution."

Some years later, around 1919, Mr. Tom Atkinson, then in his teens, recalls a Buffalo Bill 'circus' coming to Hull's Walton Street ground. Having been brought up on a farm, he was interested in the horses and wagons, which he remembers as being of the pole type with flat beds. The show was apparently in a 'Big Top' tent with a group of Indians and squaws and the central 'Cody' character galloping around firing six-shooters into the air. Nothing in this show resembles the true Wild West, especially as Cody had died two years earlier. Even at the time, to those who would know little of the real Buffalo Bill, rumours were common that of course this was an 'impostor'.

When the Wild West gave its last performance in Hull in 1904, it was sixteen years since Buffalo Bill had left the port for home aboard the Persian Monarch. This time, he headed north, for a new venue in the City of York.

## York (4th July, 1904)

While there is little information available about the Wild West in York, Independence Day must have been celebrated by American members of the show in some way, but hard liquor was not generally allowed on the showground. The site of the performances was the Knavesmire, close to the centre of the city today, better known for other equestrian pursuits. Perhaps as a concession for Independence Day, only the tents needed for human accommodation were erected that Sunday morning. Those people who chose to take a stroll in the direction of the Knavesmire saw the Wild West as few others would, Sunday being the one day that there were no performances. For those who would be attending the show, tickets were available in advance from Banks & Sons, of the Music Warehouse, Stonegate.

Early the next day, the rest of the nine acres of canvas were set up and fine weather prompted a good attendance. Eight thousand came for the afternoon show, and as it ended, rain began. It did not, however, deter another ten thousand from coming that evening.

York City Council met that Monday to discuss the Volunteer Role of Honour, the Walmgate Arc Lamp and the state of the city tramways. While some members showed a little eagerness to conclude business for the evening, 'for their own reasons', one Mr. Blakey advised that he had no wish to 'put these matters in the way of those wishing to flee to the Wild West'. Continuing, he remarked, a little sarcastically. . .

*A rare photograph showing two of the Wild West Indians on the Knavesmire, York in 1904.*

"Let's pack up and be off to the Knavesmire to witness the whirl of the lasso, the wardance of the wild 'uns and the acrobatic boundings of Bedouins".

The war-whoop of the Indians became somewhat irritating to many people for a while after the visit of the Wild West, with many of the younger men taking up the 'coi-yoi-yoi', when as one newspaper reported, 'the dry ginger had been circulated freely in sundry hotels - and when suddenly indulged in has a remarkable effect on those who have the nerves'.

## Scarborough (5th July, 1904)

Most holiday makers who walk the well-known thoroughfares of Scarborough today would be surprised indeed to know that some ninety years ago, the same streets were traversed by Sioux and Cheyenne Indians, Cossacks and cowboys, all a part of Buffalo Bill's Wild West.

The distance from York to Scarborough is forty-two miles but was certainly no exceptional distance for the show to travel between stands. Train number one came in at three o' clock in the morning, consisting of eighteen stock and sleeping cars. Train number two towed a total of seventeen vehicles, mainly flat cars, and number three had fourteen stock and sleeping cars. On arrival at the seaside town, the three trains were shunted into Gallows Close goods yard and the de-training swung smoothly into operation.

The big draught horses, hitched in teams of four, six or eight, hauled heavily laden wagons down North Marine Road towards the tram terminus which was situated at the end of the highway. Turning down Burniston Road, the wagons rolled through a hole cut into the hedge which surrounded the showground. Large, privately owned hotels now abound in the area, close to the large swimming pool near the north shore, but at the time of the Wild West this was the edge of town. An hour before the first wagons reached the ground, a team of men were measuring and marking the field for the various parts of the Wild West, right down to where each road vehicle would unload. Apart from the whip

carried by the driver of the Deadwood Stagecoach, and then mainly for effect, no other was used upon the horses, each animal controlled by light handling of the reins and the voice of the teamster. Much was made by the press and public alike of the preparations carried out by those erecting the canvas, but most interest again was in the Indians who, within an hour of reaching the field, had set up their teepees in the north west corner and covered the ground with fresh straw. Used to inquisitive noses poked through the flaps of their lodges, the Indians generally treated the public with a good nature. They were also seen to be on excellent terms with their fellow performers, engaging in 'rough fun' with men of other nations, and even some of the onlookers. The public were still curious about the Russians and the Japanese due to the serious events unfolding at home. Scarborians noted them to be 'moody-looking, as though oppressed by a weight of thought'.

Eleven thousand attended the afternoon show in fine, warm weather. They marvelled at the horsemen, especially the Cossacks who hung in every possible position from the saddles of their galloping horses. They enjoyed immensely the Mexican ropers, the cowboys struggling with their bucking mounts, the battles and the military drills. After his recent accident, much relief was shown by the crowd at the successful leap of the cowboy cyclist, but still the star was Buffalo Bill, eliciting much applause from the audience upon his entry into the arena.

To most people who saw the show that day, the two hours passed all too quickly, and before many more hours went by, the Wild West had gone once more, the sound of gunfire and war cries still ringing in the ears of those who had witnessed it.

From Scarborough, the Wild West left Yorkshire, and moving north played at Stockton-on-Tees, Middlesbrough, West Hartlepool, Newcastle and Sunderland. Then north again into Scotland where it stayed, visiting many of the larger towns and cities until 15th September when it returned to England, at Penrith. From here the show meandered south again, into Lancashire and finally back into Yorkshire, making a one day stand at Skipton.

## Skipton (10th October, 1904)

Cody was by now longing for his home on the North Platte and looking forward to returning to Nebraska. Rumours were circulating of a tour of mainland Europe the following year, but the 1904 season was drawing to a close and the Wild West was preparing to return home within two weeks. All of the advertising announced that this was the final time that the show would be seen in the United Kingdom. Cow Pasture Parlour, a field near the railway station, proved an ideal place for the show at Skipton. Arriving from Burnley the day before, the area around the engine sheds early on the morning of Sunday 9th October assumed the usual combination of smooth organisation on the part of the show people, and excited bustle from sightseers who had risen early to catch every detail.

The weather was favourable and attendance on the afternoon of Monday 10th was excellent. English contingents were strongly applauded. Roosevelt was now President, and the squadron of Rough Riders, veterans of the Spanish-American War, achieved a keen interest. The cowboy cyclist was such a novelty that many thought it the most sensational part of the programme. This might seem strange to us today when there are so many bicycles to be seen on the streets, but in 1904, horse transport was more common and such a feat by pedal power would certainly have been unusual.

The advertisement in Skipton's Craven Herald was one of the largest to be used in the newspapers, measuring eight inches deep by four wide. Perhaps to catch the maximum attention of the public, the advert details every aspect of the show in the florid manner of the period. The Craven Herald office at 38, High Street, Skipton, was also the place where tickets were available away from the showground.

## Harrogate (11th October, 1904)

Forty people had preceded the Wild West many days before the show arrived in Harrogate. These were the crew of the Advance Booking and Publicity Car, the railway vehicle known to the show people simply as 'the Advance', or 'Number One', where number one was the number on the carriage. Details of the operation of this section of the show are explained in another chapter, but its function was to check that all arrangements were in order and ensure that maximum publicity was maintained by way of flyers, posters, handbills and newspaper articles etc.

Goodrick's Fields on the Otley Road were decided upon to house the Wild West for the one day stand, with George Musgrove's Pianoforte Warehouse of 34, Parliament Street, as the ticket centre. The newspapers enticed the public with evocative advertising, embellished with illustrations of an Indian Chief, and a rousing picture 'Custer's Last Rally', all headed of course with a portrait of Buffalo Bill.

It should be clear to the reader that the Wild West was second to none in its methods of organisation and treatment of men and animals. Thanks to the Harrogate press we are able to learn a little more of life backstage.

As well as the forty people of the Advance, the main show employed approximately six hundred and eighty. We can see that the management endeavoured to provide good working conditions for its staff, with good pay, free time and more than adequate catering arrangements. At least two kinds of meat were always available and sometimes three, together with fresh vegetables and bread. In return, workers needed little encouragement and few spoken words of command from the heads of department to perform their duties. Spectators often commented on the lack of noise and fuss during the erection of the showground. Sub division of labour was well defined and no one was in doubt as to his duties and consequently the whole operation ran like clockwork. During the whole of the 1904 season, only one man reported sick, due to a hereditary tuberculosis condition.

The horses were equally well treated, stabled on fresh ground with six tons of fresh straw distributed daily, along with the same amount of hay. One hundred and thirty men were employed in the stables alone and each horse, whether a show or draught animal, was groomed regularly. In Cody's opinion, it was better to care for each animal than to buy fresh horses.

There was a story about the Wild West horses. An angler needed coarse, white tail hair for fishing and tried to find a supply in the show's stables. He could not find one strong enough due to the fact that the animals were so well kept. During the 1904 season, only one horse was sick.

### Castleford (12th October, 1904)

The papers stated that during the day of the Wild West all roads led to Lock Lane, where the show was held. Arriving from Harrogate at around six o' clock, it was received by large crowds of onlookers yet again, many of whom followed the long procession of wagons down Aire Street. Despite the suggestion that money was scarce at the time in the north of England, patrons began to arrive several hours before the beginning of each performance.

From the overture to the final revue, the audiences were enthralled and spoke of it for days afterward. They marvelled at Johnny Baker's shooting, hitting targets with precision from every conceivable position. As in other places the unusual was keenly appreciated, especially the cowboy cyclist and the life-saving drill. Every child became Buffalo bill in the playgrounds in the weeks that followed, and for many the memories remained with them until they in turn told their own children of the day that the Wild West came to Castleford.

### Barnsley (13th October, 1904))

The canvas mushroomed on the Queens Grounds that Thursday morning, a perfect site for such a large exhibition. Although cool, the weather remained reasonable and many took advantage of the railway excursions, trams and wagonettes to travel to the showground. The police were reinforced with special constables to control the crowds, who on the whole were very well behaved.

Circuses had visited before but this was no ordinary show, and excitement had been high for several days beforehand. What the audiences perceived that day was real, giving exactly what the posters promised, a congress of rough riders from the corners of a world that was disappearing fast. Cody did not make the mistake of splitting his show as others had done in the past, each touring in the guise of a larger concern. Indeed the touring Wild West was larger than that presented at Earle's Court, a fact that the 'Advance' capitalised on.

Also new for the current season was a game played by two teams of horsemen, usually Indians and cowboys. The game was a kind of horse football, the ball being six feet in diameter, and the idea being to shove it by force through a goal at each end of the arena. Apparently the Indians entered into the sport with much gusto and rough fun.

The demise of Custer was still a popular event, and the Barnsley audience found the performance very dramatic. Due to the US 7th Cavalry being wiped out to a man, historically, we have mainly the accounts given later by Indian protagonists, and the truth is somewhat different to the picture normally shown us by Hollywood. In the nineteen eighties, archaeological work carried out on the site gave a more realistic scenario. It is now generally believed that Custer's force was split by the Indians, Custer and about fifty troopers defending a low hill and being despatched quite early in the engagement. The remainder ceased to be an efficient fighting unit and attempted to withdraw, the remnants probably being finally surrounded and killed in a deep ravine not far from the Big Horn River. Around two thousand artefacts have so far been unearthed, including the remains of troopers who died there. The facial bones of Custer's scout, Michael 'Mitch' Boyer, have been identified. Boyer was a multi-lingual half Sioux who is attributed with warning Custer against entering the Big Horn Valley and potential disaster. Dying with the famous General that day were many of Buffalo Bill's friends, including Custer's brother, Tom. The story of a single cavalry horse being found on the battlefield seems unlikely, as no self-respecting Sioux would leave such a valuable prize.

## Huddersfield (14th October, 1904)

Longley Park was the place where the Wild West was next to be seen and tickets could be pre-booked at J. Wood & Sons, the Music Warehouse at 67, New Street. The return home to America was now in sight and the Advance Booking railway car was on its way back to the winter quarters at Stoke-on-Trent, having completed its task while the last few stands were being played. Buffalo Bill, now portly and in middle age, was engaged in various projects in America, including the irrigation of the Big Horn basin, with financial help from the Government, and was looking forward to becoming more personally involved.

De-training began at six-thirty and with only a few more performances still to go the weather had turned cold. The evening show progressed as normal but the cowboy cyclist could not perform due to frost. Built of iron with a hardwood track the ramp which the cyclist used would have been very dangerous under these conditions. The programme made it clear that the act could be abandoned in the event of poor weather.

The leader of the Cossacks was introduced, wearing the Cross of St. George, presented by the Czar for bravery at Plevna, during the Russian-Turkish War. Two of the US Cavalrymen had served in the Franco-Prussian War, while among the English horsemen were those who had served in India, Egypt and South Africa. Other Americans had fought in the Philippines, and introduced by name was Tom Isabelle, who had fired the first shot at San Juan Hill and was wounded seven times in the action. This then, was the calibre of men who rode before the audiences at Huddersfield.

As the show ended, 175 workers quietly began to manage the canvas, and within half an hour most had been taken down, ready for packing onto the wagons. Reaching the waiting trains, haul up teams dragged the vehicles aboard the flat cars. Later, the horses embarked; each walking up the ramp with no trouble, and going to its own familiar place in the stock car, without need for urging from the grooms.

One final note on the visit to Huddersfield concerns the inclusion of an article in the Huddersfield Examiner on 15th October, entitled 'An unrehearsed scene at Buffalo Bills'. In these days of relatively rudimentary medicine, we find the purveyors of Dr. William's Pink Pills for Pale People using the Wild West for its own devices. What is in fact an advertisement for the preparation, the article blatantly pretends to be a factual piece of journalism. It is some nine inches by one column long, including a sketch of 'cowboy Canham', who apparently prescribed the pills after a fall from his horse in Newcastle. We can only guess at the possibility of Canham's misadventure, or even to his existence, but the pills were cited to be beneficial for anything from back pain to constipation, and counterfeit versions of the product were also warned against. A nice touch. Such advertisements were quite common, cashing in on any item or event of interest to the public, and several lines are usually read before the reader is alerted to the true meaning of the article. Doubtless, some were taken in and assumed such pieces to have been genuine, when connected to bona fide events.

Leaving Huddersfield, the Wild West moved to Ashton-under-Lyne, then Glossop, Stockport, Northwick and Macclesfield for one day stands, and finally Hanley on 21st October, close to the winter quarters at Stoke. Shortly thereafter, the show returned to America but in 1905, crossed the Atlantic again for a last tour of France, Italy, Austria, Germany, Hungary, Luxembourg, Belgium and a short stay in Russia. The tour ended in France once more on October 30th, 1906. Cody and the Wild West were now enjoying their last golden years.

# VITAL STATISTICS

*Canvas, Cable and Cowboys, Pickles, Powder and Popcorn. Supplying the Wild West.*

In both European and American tours, plans had to be made many months ahead in order to maximise the number of people that would be able to attend the show. This was especially the case in America so that seasonal variations (such as harvest time) could be considered, when the public would have more money to spend. Also, the Wild West was not the only travelling show and routes were planned to beat rivals to favoured venues. This tactic could deny revenue to a competitor or even put him out of business permanently. It was also common sense to avoid areas recently visited. Because of its size, planning was vital to the running of the Wild West in every way and forward organisation helped to ensure that problems in transportation and supply were kept to a minimum.

## General Staff

Even from the early days of Buffalo Bill's Wild West, the supply of everyday needs to the show must have been awesome. In the later years when it had increased several fold, it would have been trebly so. The route book for 1899 (US tour) gives a good idea as to what and who would have been involved.

The publication still showed Buffalo Bill to be the President with Nate Salsbury as Vice-President and Major John Burke as general Manager. (The reader should note that the route book was published two years after the involvement of Bailey). Two directors for the tour were shown, James Bailey and W. W. Cole, with Louis E. Cooke as General Agent. Next came two business managers, one for Cody (Jule Keen), and one for Bailey and Cole (Ernest Cooke). The two Cookes may have been related. Jule Keen also served as Treasurer for Cody and Salsbury, while Fred B. Hutchinson served in the same role for Bailey and Cole. The two sides of the partnership also had their own respective secretaries, L. E. Decker for Cody and Joseph F. Quaid for Bailey.

Director of Entertainment was Johnny Baker, who, as we have seen, also starred in the show. He was again referred to as Arenic Director, and apart from Cody himself, had the final say in the staging of the show. There was also a Superintendent of Grounds by the name of Henry Barnum. Surely it would be too much of a coincidence if the man was not a relative of the great Barnum (then deceased), and likely attained his post via James Bailey. A reference to Managers of Privileges, Messrs. Drew and Campbell, completed the higher echelon of administration.

There followed a list of General Staff. These were still managers in their own right with relevant responsibilities :-

| | |
|---|---|
| John Baker | Arenic Director |
| John McLoughlin | Master of Transportation |
| Dan Taylor | Master Mechanic |
| M.B. Bailey | Supt. of Electric Lights |
| Jake Platt | Supt. of Canvas |
| Charles Evans | Supt. of baggage Stock |
| W.W. Reedy | Supt. of Bronco Stock |
| C.W. Ramsey | Supt. of Confectionery Dept. |
| Wm. Sweeney | Leader of Cowboy Band |
| Wm. McCune | Officer of the day |
| Morris Kern | Principal Door tender |
| J.W. Rogers | Detective |
| J.J. McCarthy | Orator |
| Louis Decker | Mail Carrier |
| John Noble | Head car Porter |
| Keen & Langan | Caterers |
| M. Martin | Head Waiter |
| John Stacks | Parade Wardrobe |
| Chas. Wichelhausen | Properties |
| Wm. Smith | Ammunition |

Some of the foregoing may seem trivial posts at first glance. However, it does show that more importance was given to some aspects of the Wild West than we might expect. The street parades, for example, in that someone was made responsible for the costumes for that event. Apart from the de-training of the show at a new venue, eagerly watched by the residents, the parade was the show's first contact with potential patrons, and a good impression was vital to persuade them to visit the grounds as paying customers.

The importance of the railways to the show is dealt with elsewhere, but we can see in the above, the inclusion of Head Car Porter. Once the company had embarked upon the trains, almost everything became the responsibility of this man, from shoe shines to sleeping accommodation. We can see how vital were the stockmen, and due to the great numbers of horses used, they were broken down into responsibilities for draught and show animals, each with their own supervisors and each in its own way crucial to the running of the Wild West.

## Advertising and Publicity

Next came the Publicity Department, most of which travelled many days ahead of the show in the Advance Advertising (railway) Car, known as the 'Advance', or 'Number One'. Generally speaking, Major Burke oversaw the operations of the publicity department, but Louis E. Cooke, whom we have previously seen as General Tour Agent, doubled as the General Advance Manager. More specifications concerning the Advance railway car can be found in the transportation chapter of this book, but its everyday use can be dealt with here.

The Advance was a very efficient and important part of the Wild West system, working under an internal manager (in 1899 - P.S. Mattox). Under him was a Boss Bill poster with ten men whose job it was, in only one day usually, to paste up around 6,000 - 8,000 sheets, to advertise a one day presentation of the Wild West. Casual labour was sometimes used, and as early as 1892, there could be as many as forty bill posters at work. Also part of the team were a Boss Lithographer with three lithographers, a

*'Number One'. The advance booking car, in B & B Livery.*

secretary, a programmer and two layers-out, making a total staff of around twenty persons, full time. The Advance also had its own Car Porter, and travelled ahead of the show by a set number of performances, preparing the way and travelling with scheduled trains. Apart from advertising duties, personnel were responsible for checking (and sometimes finding) the showground, obtaining the appropriate licenses and ensuring continuity of supplies.

*A two-colour Wild West poster.*

For the later US tours, there was also a second Advance Booking Car, known as Number Two, the Excursion Department, with its own complement of staff. Part of the staff of Number Two was a section called the 'Opposition Brigade', a manager and four men employed to counter any advertising by rival shows. This was possibly a direct influence of James Bailey and his circus mentality. Obtaining prime venues had been so important that competing circuses had come to physical violence on occasion, and were certainly not adverse to replacing a rival's poster with their own.

While the posters were the principal form of addressing the public, newspaper adverts were also important. Less colourful, they were also a way of reaching a large number of people in a short time, and usually included a list of performers and events. The advertising department carried their own blocks for the adverts in several sizes, needing only a minimum of work by the newspapers, adding dates and times, before insertion and printing. These adverts were usually carried in the press around a week before the show arrived. Some of the larger ones carried illustrations depicting the various aspects of the show. There were many of these and included pictures of Buffalo Bill himself, Arabs, Cavalry, Indians, military equestrians, bucking broncos, buffaloes, and even a scenario of Custer's Last Stand.

Without a doubt, however, it was the colourful posters which captured the imagination of potential patrons, and really portrayed the spirit of the Wild West. Even for the first visit in 1887/8 the Wild West's stock of posters was substantial indeed, and so many were posted around the capital that one London newspaper, The Globe, was prompted to verse:-

*I may walk it, or bus it, or Hansom it, still. . .*
*I am faced by the features of Buffalo Bill. . .*
*Every hoarding is plastered from East-end to West. . .*
*Wit' his hat, coat and countenance, lovelocks and vest.*

The posters are now considered some of the best examples of the work of lithographers and style artists of the period. So lucrative was the work for travelling shows that, in the US especially,

*A Press Advertisement.*

*A Press Advertisement.*

some printers carried specialist artists who were responsible only for certain aspects of the original artwork. For example, one artist might be employed to concentrate on just horses while another would cover the performers. The posters were made to a pre-ordained size. A one sheet bill was 28" wide by 42" high, and around this measurement the larger hoardings would be calculated, consisting of many butt-jointed sheets. These were usually in the scale of 2, 3, 6, 9, 12, 16, 20, 24, 28 and 32 sheet combinations, but could occasionally be much longer with up to 168 sheets, covering an area of 9 feet high by 143 feet long. Such monsters were even more unique in that they portrayed one major scene, rather than just a series of smaller ones joined together. Some of the big circus poster presentations did just that. The big Wild West posters often had 4 sheet text panels at each end, known as 'opening' and 'signature' panels. Separate slips showing the correct date and place could be pasted over to tailor the bills to the venue. There were also smaller half sheets, quarter sheets and playbills that could be used to take advantage of sites such as telegraph poles, etc., the smallest being a simple one colour press on coloured paper. Occasionally, special size posters were produced, pennant shaped or banner types.

Bearing in mind the cost of modern day mediums such as television, advertising to the Wild West was relatively inexpensive and was probably offset by revenue obtained from advertisers allowed into the official programmes. To give an idea of the cost of the posters can only be approximate for various reasons, but on one occasion for example, the cost of a 108 sheet billboard was $10. Usually between 1000 and 1500 were ordered at a time.

The role of the 'Advance' was varied. Besides its normal employment, it could be workshop, office and stockroom. It was cleverly fitted out with work tops, drawers, cupboards and also drop-down bunks for the staff. The fully fitted office was at one end of the vehicle and had its own window, but the main length of the car was given to work surfaces, slightly wider than a standard poster with a central walkway. At the opposite end of the carriage was a large boiler for making paste. Built in the American style, there was a surprising amount of headroom and

*A recent postcard reproducing original artwork used by the Wild West.*

the whole would have been lit by oil lamps, and natural light where possible. Under the centre of the car, between the two bogie wheel arrangements, was a large box, in which would be stored the ladders, pots and other necessary equipment. The car itself also served to promote the Wild West in its own right, painted white and being colourfully decorated in circus style lettering, informing the public of the coming of :-

'The World's Greatest and Grandest Educational Show'
'The Wonders of the Western Wilds - brought to the doors
of the East together with a
Grand Military Tournament by the
Rough Riders of All Nations'

BUFFALO BILL'S WILD WEST
And
CONGRESS OF ROUGH RIDERS OF THE WORLD

ADVANCE ADVERTISING CAR

There were also painted shields around the doors and windows
with such mottoes as,

'Truthful. . .Moral. . .Instructive'
'Advance Advertising Car'

and other slogans belying the car's origins with Barnum &
Bailey's
'Greatest Show on Earth'.

### The Showground

The 1899 Route book shows that the Wild West employed two full time ticket sellers in the main ticket wagon, which would have been situated near the main entrance. There were also three others working the nearby area. In the local town, there would also be a small portable kiosk erected, known as the 'downtown office'. An orator would stand with the kiosk to draw in crowds as in the manner of modern markets. Three reserved seat ticket collectors were also employed and came under the control of Jule Keen, Buffalo Bill's business manager and treasurer.

The main entrance to the Wild West was controlled by four door-tenders, and in addition there was a head usher with two assistants. The reserved seats had two tenders of their own and a further nine ushers. The better seats and boxes also had a team of ten attendants, a director and a wardrobe attendant to look after cloaks and hats. Another door-tender was responsible for the sideshow.

*Souvenir belt buckle sold on the showgrounds.*

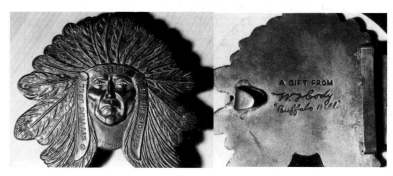

*Wild West postcard.*

*The 'Rough Rider'.*

Official programmes during the Wild West's final tour of the UK were published by The Partington Advertising Company and printed by Weiner's Ltd. of London, and are generally dealt with in another section of this book. They are today quite rare and keenly sought after by collectors, but they were not the only souvenir sold on the grounds. Buffalo Bill's official autobiography was available, there were Wild West scrapbooks, figurines and postcards, bookmarks and 'genuine' Indian bows and arrows and peace pipes. Many souvenirs were everyday items upon which the Wild West stamped a Buffalo Bill portrait, and were sold via a mock up of a log cabin or ground vendors. Confectionery was also on sale and the Route Book of 1899 details a Superintendent of Confectionery, with an assistant, and one more in charge of supplies. Items sold under this category would include toffee apples, hard candy and especially popcorn. It has been said that it was the Wild West that was responsible for introducing popcorn to the western world, and this may be so. Beer was also available, along with lemonade and soda-pop, the show at this time having its own carbonating equipment.

An especially important feature of the Wild West was its ability to give shows at night with the aid of early floodlighting. The electrical department had its own superintendent, chief electrician, chief engineer and six assistants. Additionally, there were two firemen, two others to deal with the calcium lighting and a further two workers dealing with chandeliers.

The twenty-four main arena floodlights were of a carbon arc type of around 4,000 candlepower, and mounted on poles along each of the long sides, in groups of four. Two more picked out the backdrop. Due to the limited generating capacity, only about half were ever used at one time. To eliminate strong shadows, special reflectors were designed by the superintendent of the electrical department, M. B. Bailey. Three searchlights, mounted on a platform at the opposite end to the backdrop, were also utilised to pick out areas of drama and personalities for the audience. Two of these lights projected 25,000 candlepower and the other 8,000, and again were of the carbon arc design. They were also useful in the trick shooting events to follow the targets when thrown into the air.

Seventy-seven lamps of 2,000 candlepower were also needed to illuminate the grounds at night, and a further 800 at 16 candlepower, were needed for the performer's tents, stables, etc. Yet another 400 at 16 candlepower were used for the grandstands. At half past six, the ground lights were turned on and the grandstands were illuminated at seven-thirty, shortly before the beginning of the show at eight.

The Wild West boasted the largest privately owned generating plant at the time, and it was certainly needed. The plant consisted of two Morin Climax, vertical, water tube boilers of 300 horsepower each. A Worthington Duplex boiler feed pump helped to build a constant pressure of 135 pounds per square inch, and in case of a breakdown, a Korting Universal Injector was fitted. Two 250 horsepower, cross-compound, non condensing Ball engines transmitted power via four sixteen inch, double leather belts to four 80 kilowatt Edison DC generators which operated at 125 volts. The Wild West was proud indeed of these mighty engines, including them in the street parades, and even made a feature of them on some of the posters.

**Raising the Canvas**

Once the Wild West arrived at a venue, the detraining of equipment would begin immediately. First off the first train would be everything needed to transform the showground into a small town. Teams of draught horses would convey tons of canvas, ropes, stakes, shackles, pulleys and hammers to the allotted place, which could sometimes be quite a distance away.

Ideally, the ground needed to be a flat area of around eleven acres. There needed to be good access for the public in order for the show to be viable, and rent imposed by the authorities should be reasonable. For both humans and animals, a good supply of fresh water was essential. For these reasons, except under rare circumstances, the sites found were normally found on the outskirts of towns and cities.

Unlike circuses, The Wild West performed in the open air. This was mainly due to the many shooting acts where a canvas roof would have quickly been shot to pieces. As the advertising stated, shows took place in any weather, rain or shine. This was certainly true and only on rare occasions was the performance cancelled. In order to avail the audience of shelter, a three sided, covered grandstand was erected, having two long sides of 320 feet, and one short one (end) of 150 feet. The other short side was the backdrop and entrance for performers. Seating accommodation was available at varying prices for up to 15,000 people.

Besides the main arena there were dining tents, stable tents, accommodation and sleeping quarters, utility tents, a barbers, a blacksmith, a side-show and souvenir stalls, and areas for the buffalo and other livestock. Behind the backdrop, an enclosed area was needed to organise the entry of each act and therefore needed to be large enough to turn a stagecoach and a team of six mules. Bearing in mind that many venues were one day stands, it is not surprising that an average working day was generally around sixteen hours. Most of the canvas structures could be erected within two hours of reaching the showground. In all, around 23,000 yards of canvas, 20 miles of rope and cable, and well over 1,000 stakes were needed. Up to 175 roustabouts and specialist workers were employed.

As the canvas wagons were unloaded on the ground, the first task was to mark out the sections, although over years of experience this became virtually unnecessary, everyone knowing areas and routine by heart. Immediately, the dining tent was erected and cooks began to prepare breakfast while work continued. As food became ready, usually within forty minutes, some workers ate, their initial tasks completed, and another section took over.

Four teams erected the grandstand, bracing the canvas between poles. Again referring to the 1899 Route Book, it shows the Canvas Department as having a total of thirty-nine staff. Additionally, there was a superintendent, two assistants and a supervisor each for the horse and dressing room tents. Then there were five side-show canvas men with a supervisor and an inside man. Three sail makers were employed to repair and keep the canvas in shape, sometimes working while the show was in transit.

As the grandstand took shape, the seat teams moved in. There were three teams of eighteen men, with a supervisor and an assistant, each having its own area of responsibility and each man with a specific task. Once the supervisors and assistants had marked out the seat positions, planking was laid in place and levelled. Men known as 'stringer setters' held stair risers in place, while 'toe-pin drivers' pegged the stringers at the front end. At the back of the construction, 'jack setters' positioned 'A' frames to support the stringers. Levels were finally re-checked, and if necessary blocked up by the 'block boy'. It may seem a complicated procedure, but as each knew his job perfectly it was quick and efficient.

A canvas back wall completed the grandstand to protect the audience from weather and, theoretically at least, to keep out non-payers. While this was going on, other teams were employed in erecting the other tents and preparing the showground for the performance. Although accommodation was provided for performers on the grounds during an extended stay, some preferred to sleep on the trains if they were close by. This happened more often when inclement weather meant a waterlogged ground.

Another large section of canvas to be erected was the backdrop, which added another dimension to the action in the arena. These were by no means as elaborate as those used during extended indoor engagements but were, if only because of their size, impressive, and needed 300lbs of paint to render the scene. These huge sheets of canvas were rigged in three sections, held between poles by ropes. Normally there would be two scenery screens, one behind the other, each of which could be drawn back to allow the entry of performers. Two operators were in charge of the left and right curtains, and a further four that were needed for the centre. Presumably, these men would help with other activities as part of their everyday workload, as they would only be needed on the backdrop during showtime.

Teams of Jack-hammer men pounded in the larger stakes with perfect timing. It was said that Sitting Bull liked to watch the hammer men at work, and sometimes took part himself for a while. To take up the stakes, they were first loosened with a hammer. A piece of equipment like a large, wheeled crowbar was then used to prise them up, the axle serving as a fulcrum.

Buffalo Bill had his own tent on the grounds, with a shield-mounted buffalo head adorning the apex. It was well furnished with carpets, photographs and easy chairs, like a well kept drawing room. Often, distinguished visitors to the camp were invited inside for something stronger than coffee. Cody also had his own railway car, equally well furnished. Annie Oakley shared a tent with her husband and manager, Frank Butler, and was particularly adept in making her canvas accommodation comfortable, although star performers in the Wild west were allowed more leeway in personal items transported with the show. One very useful piece of equipment that Annie used was a trunk in which she could store her costumes without folding, and when opened it doubled as a dresser with a small mirror.

Apart from the senior management and star performers, who had their own accommodation, general staff and cast members slept two to a tent. These tents were about twelve feet square, and were complete with folding beds and tables, and a travelling box for each person containing their personal items. Normally, when travelling, the bulk of personal belongings were only brought from the trains on Sundays when there were no performances. Many of the Indians in the show preferred their traditional teepees, but some preferred the tents, and when close by, like other performers, liked to sleep aboard the trains.

For the general cast there was a dressing tent behind and to one side of the backdrop. In the centre was a large tank with drinking water and two smaller ones for washing. A rope was put up near the inside wall, upon which performers could hang their clothing and equipment and formed a kind of screen for those who wished it.

Two blacksmiths, given the title of 'Wild West Blacksmiths', in the Route books, also had their own tent and were kept constantly busy. Apart from shoeing horses, these men would also keep the wagons, machinery and props in first class repair. Some British newspapers reported two blacksmith tents and a harness repair tent. A large separate tent was required for the show and draught horses, the animals secured both around the inside perimeter and within a central loop.

The electric light department had its own canvas, as did the wardrobe and properties department (with five operatives), and in later years the mechanics and working men's department. The lady riders were also accommodated separately behind the backdrop, as was the ammunition store with its superintendent and three assistants.

**Food and Drink**

Many newspaper reports, in describing the activities of the Wild West in their region, found the scale of catering for such a huge enterprise almost as interesting as the show itself. Many equated the task to the provisioning of an army, and rightly so, publishing the long list of comestibles for both humans and animals.

The Yorkshire Evening Post (Leeds) of 28th September 1903 states:-

'The five hundred horses and eight hundred men connected with the exhibition are all fed on the premises. The ten cooks and sixty waiters distribute something like 1,400lbs. of meat daily in addition to 7cwt. of potatoes, 450 lbs. of bread, and 30cwt. of miscellaneous vegetables. About 2,100 meals are served daily in a large marquee where 500 can sit down together. Colonel Cody always takes food with his staff.'

Some reports state that two dining marquees were used, and this was possibly true in later years when the show was at its largest. When arriving at a new showground, the range wagon was one of the first to arrive and breakfast was ready within forty minutes.

The Wild West was totally self contained, and around 1900, the cost of a day's provisions was around $400, not an inconsiderable sum for the period. Three meals per day were provided and due to the strict time schedules of the show, had to be punctual. Breakfast was served between 7.30am and 9.00am, lunch between 12.30 and 1.30pm, and dinner between 6.00 and 7.30pm. Culinary standards were excellent, as witnessed by the many reporters welcomed and entertained by the Wild West, who marvelled at the 'white cloth and plate service'. This was served with the regularity of a first class restaurant. Once the tables were laid with cloths, individual plates were placed upside down with a cup and saucer on top and knife and fork at the side. Immediately upon taking their places at the tables, the cast and crew were served with hot coffee or tea.

On one occasion, newspapermen invited to breakfast enjoyed grilled steak and potatoes, bread and strong coffee, followed by strawberries and cream, and upon their emerging from the dining tent were astounded that the grounds had been turned into a canvas city while they ate.

The number of people actually involved in preparing the food varied over the years, but there were usually between five and seven cooks, including a camp fire (barbecue) attendant, and two pastry cooks. The 1899 Route Book lists a head butcher and ten assistants, a head and an assistant waiter, and if newspaper reports are accurate, up to sixty waiters. The waiters were responsible for specific tables and duties. For example, there might be three looking after table number six (English and German soldiers), and one specifically for serving coffee. The three workmen's tables ( eight, nine and ten ), needed six waiters and two coffee boys. In all there were usually ten long tables provided, with managerial staff occupying number one. Also in the dining tent was a large distilled water tank for drinking, and it was noted by some reporters that the Indians always took a drink of water before leaving.

Two dessert boys completed the team, with two dishwashers, a laundryman and a night-lunch waiter for evening workers such as the two night watchmen.

To prepare the food, several options were available. The Wild West had its own 26 foot long range wagon with four fitted stoves and preparation tops. This wagon was designed by he catering manager, D. Ballard, and while fairly small with only one fire source, provided facilities to feed a vast number of people very quickly. Steam tables were also available, served by their own boiler, and several 100 gallon cauldrons could be utilised. Food was also served outside under the right conditions, and campfire or barbecued food was sold to the public on the showground. During the tours of 1903/4 meat was shipped daily from Liverpool for use the following day, and held in a refrigerating van.

While tea and coffee were freely available at any time, no hard liquor was allowed on the showground, and drunkenness of any kind was not tolerated. Few, if any reports exist of this law being broken. The tea and coffee were dispensed from huge urns, made brilliant by much polishing and for the benefit of the staff and performers, there was also a provision wagon known as the 'Pie Car'. Under the control of the Manager of Privileges, this was a mobile store from which they could buy sundry items such as newspapers, soap and cigarettes at reasonable cost.

The animals with the show also needed a considerable amount of supplies. On average, 10 tons of hay, 5 tons of straw, 350 bushels of oats, 200 sacks of bran, 25 sacks of maize, and 2 bags of rock salt were required per week. To oversee the horses the Wild West employed a superintendent and fifteen men.

## Legal and Binding

Those employed by the Wild West as performers were required to sign a contract prior to the opening of the season, which clearly informed the artist of his or her duties within the context of the show. The management's care for its people was far in advance of the time and withheld two weeks pay until the end of the season, to ensure that the employee had enough money to find his way home.

The contract absolved the Wild West from any responsibility for injury to the performers, but by the same token considerable care was given to anyone being hurt in the show.

On the reverse side of the document the artist was presented with a list of regulations which had to be adhered to. Cleanliness and neatness were essential at all times, and especially so in such confined spaces as the railway carriages. Costumes were always the responsibility of the performer and had to be ready for each performance. Good conduct and ' gentlemanly manner' was stressed, with no leeway given for gambling, fighting or drinking. Smiling at, winking at or generally eyeing-up lady members of the audience was also not considered conducive to the spirit of the show and trading in Indian artefacts or clothing was a total taboo.

During performances, the artistes were not to loiter anywhere they were not supposed to be, and hinder others in the execution of their duties. Sleeping with boots on and shotguns was also forbidden, and apart from Indians who used them in their section of the show, no dogs were allowed, or other pets. In addition to the dressing trunk of 18" x 18" x 24", a personal box of the same measurement was allowed, and these were brought from the trains on Sundays only.

Roustabouts and workmen, although employed on a less formal basis were still given much consideration within their employment. Food, conditions and pay were good by any standards, and many stayed with the show for some time.

# FINALE

*The decline of Buffalo Bill's Wild West.*
*What happened to the performers, the show, and Buffalo Bill.*

As the Wild West completed its European tour and returned to the United States in 1907, the death of James Bailey was the first of a sequence of events which would lead to the decline and eventual termination of the show. Cody had disagreed with many of Bailey's circus-style innovations, such as the side-show, but he had been to some extent free to maintain the general western theme of the presentation, a certain amount of autonomy, and not least, temporary financial relief. Bad weather and other problems meant that the last European tour had not been a success financially. Also, Cody had risked his money poorly in many ill-advised business projects, and needed to borrow heavily in order to keep the show going. Besides the two thirds interest that he had sold to Bailey he had taken an additional loan of $12,000 from the latter. Buffalo Bill always insisted that the loan had been repaid, despite the absence of a receipt. The Bailey estate insisted upon repayment, and so hoping for good profits when the following season began, Cody borrowed from friends and mortgaged some personal property. He rented equipment and winter quarters from Ringling Brothers, who now owned the Barnum & Bailey show, and managed to take the Wild West on tour again in the United States.

Due to his debts to the Bailey estate, Cody looked for long term investors in the Wild West and found one in the larger than life character of Pawnee Bill (Gordon Lillee), another showman in a similar mould to himself. In the early days of the Wild West, Pawnee Bill had been employed by Cody in the show, then leaving to start his own and become a serious competitor, until a savage advertising war between the two enterprises put him out of business. However, it is a tribute to Pawnee Bill's tenacity that by 1890 he was back on the road with a western show once more. Competition with the Wild West was avoided when Cody's show was on tour in Europe and vice versa, and so Lillee was in a healthy position to partner Buffalo Bill when help was so badly needed. It may seem surprising that no animosity prevailed between the two, but Pawnee Bill would certainly see the advantage of being involved with the long term success of Buffalo Bill and the Wild West. In any case, Lillee bought out the interest held by the Bailey estate and made Cody an offer that would allow him to re-purchase a half interest in the show with future profits, and by 1911 he had done so.

Known from then on as 'Buffalo Bill's Wild West and Pawnee Bill's Far East', the entertainment was generally referred to as 'The Two Bills Show'. One major change only was made by Lillee, the inclusion of an item called 'A Dream of the Orient', and was basically an Arabian Nights tableau with camels, elephants, and many other attributes of the theme. To Cody this must have been something of a concession to Lillee, but at least the remainder of the show retained its western background.

*Cody at his Hunting Camp. Reproduced from the programme.*

*Cody at his Hunting Camp. Reproduced from the programme.*

By this time, Cody's thoughts were on retirement to the North Platte, and in 1910, he and Lillee announced a series of farewell tours. Audiences were keen to see the show before it finished but as Cody's profits were eaten up by his poor investments, not least his mine in Arizona, he continually needed money and the 'farewell tours' went on and on, sometimes playing to recently visited stands. This did not enhance his reputation to the paying public and consequently poor attendance in bad weather in 1911 left him broke by 1912. He looked once more for investors, and through his sister was introduced to Harry Tammen, owner of the Sells Floto Circus and part owner of the Denver Post newspaper. Tammen offered Cody a $20,000 loan over six months at 6% interest, and he accepted. Tammen, aware of competition from other circuses, by the contract merged his show with the 'Wild West and Far East' for the season of 1914. With his signature, Cody had agreed to travel with the Sells Floto Circus in 1914, and somehow also gave Tammen the rights to the name of 'Buffalo Bill'. Whether Cody had read the contract carefully enough to understand this is doubtful, but the outcome was that the ageing scout had signed away the thing that was most precious to him, his name.

*Gordon Lillee alias Pawnee Bill.*

Although Pawnee Bill expressed some anger at the combination of the shows, he agreed to complete the 1913 season, but again bad weather and poor audiences left Buffalo Bill in debt at the close of business that year. With Tammen threatening legal action, Lillee, possibly in revenge, booked the show into Denver. He must have known that Tammen's lawyers were poised there to confront Cody, and so on 13th May 1913, the show was attached. More pressure was exerted upon Cody by Tammen, who found more debts owed him and as Lillee tried to file for bankruptcy, Cody dissolved the partnership.

The Wild West was auctioned in Denver on 15th September 1913, leaving many of the cast without funds to return home. True to his reputation, Buffalo Bill did his utmost to help them as best he could.

Cody returned to his home in the Big Horn basin, down but not out. Sometime later he became involved in the fledgling movie industry, producing a series of eight short films based upon highlights of his life. Surprisingly he was again backed by Tammen. As with the Wild West, it was Cody's plan to make the films as authentic as possible, using real locations and some of the original participants. The Secretary of State for War was enthusiastic and allowed Cody to use the Pine Ridge Reservation and the Indians there, and also a detachment of six hundred cavalrymen. The films were only partly successful and Cody was obliged to travel with the Sells Floto Circus in 1914 to fulfil his agreement with Tammen. In this capacity he was required only to introduce the performance, not taking part in any of the acts. By the end of the season he was tired and ill, returning to his T.E. Ranch to recuperate. Legal wranglings with Tammen and Pawnee Bill continued, and Buffalo Bill finally agreed to fulfil his commitment for the 1915 season, appearing 366 times in 183 days. Early in 1916, he gave a lecture tour, supported by the films, and had high hopes of putting together another Wild West. However, Tammen's rights to the title, 'Buffalo Bill's Wild West' made the possibilities doubtful.

With the first World War raging in Europe and America about to enter the conflict, Cody re-shaped his ideas and approached the Chief of Staff of the US Army, Major General Scott, suggesting a 'Pageant of Preparedness', which would include a Wild West element. Seeing this as a recruitment aid, Scott approved, offering support in the shape of men and equipment. Buffalo Bill looked for backing and found it in the '101 Ranch Wild West', another travelling show owned by the Miller Brothers. The result was a curious mixture of circus, western and military spectacle in a similar but less impressive style to the recently demised Wild West. Cody's involvement was small, but he delighted in the fact that Johnny Baker and other friends had been given employment in the enterprise. Initially the grandstands were full, but toward the end of the season public interest faded and the last performance was given at Portsmouth, Virginia on 11th November.

As the events unfolded, Buffalo Bill's health had not been good. On occasion he needed help from Johnny Baker to mount his horse but as soon as the music began, he sat erect in the saddle and just like the old days, rode into the arena like a twenty-year-old. With thoughts on another season, Cody decided to visit his sister in Denver and arrived totally exhausted, both in body and mind. His sister quickly sent for Cody's wife, Louisa, his daughter, Irma, and his other sister, Julia. Seeing his family again gave Cody new heart and they all set out for Wyoming, but when the scout became ill again they returned to Denver where the doctor recommended a visit to the healing waters of Glenwood Springs. The journey there took its toll on Cody, and the doctor, certain that the showman was dying, accompanied him back to Denver once more. Most of the family had returned to the town of Cody, but were now cabled to return to his bedside, where it was then clear that Buffalo Bill was close to death.

Possibly at Louisa's insistence, Cody was baptised into the Catholic faith on 9th January. A persisting story states that when he was sure of his impending demise, Buffalo Bill looked at those about him and declared something along the lines of. . .

"Well, what the hell, let's play a few hands of cards. . .".

There may be some truth in the story but Cody's main concern was that Johnny Baker should arrive before he died. Sadly, he did not. As Baker was rushing by train to the old scout's bedside, Buffalo Bill died in his wife's arms at five minutes past noon on 10th January, 1917.

Cody's body lay in state for a day in the rotunda of Colorado's State Capitol building. Outside, a military band played and his horse stood tethered with the showman's empty boots secured in the stirrups. Later, the body was placed in a coffin and taken to a crypt until the next spring, then to a prepared grave on Lookout Mountain, where a further funeral service was held. Buffalo Bill had apparently wanted to be buried in his town of Cody but with little funds available, Louisa had been forced to accept Tammen's offer to provide a suitable grave in Colorado.

*The Deadwood coach as it appears today in the Buffalo Bill Historical Museum.*

Six weeks after Cody's death, Major Burke died in Washington DC, and was buried in that city with honours by the Elk's Lodge. In October 1918, Cody's daughter Irma and her husband died of influenza. Louisa died of a heart attack in October 1921. Johnny Baker continued to tour, lecturing on Buffalo Bill and initiating a museum dedicated to him. He died in a hospital in Denver in 1931 and at his own request, his ashes were scattered near the graves of Cody's children at Rochester, New York.

Texas Jack Omahundro died in 1880, and 'Doc' Carver died in Sacramento, California on 31st August, 1927. His body was taken to Winslow, Illinois, and buried beside that of his mother on September 5th. As we have already seen in the previous pages, Nate Salsbury died on Christmas Eve 1902, and was buried at Woodlawn cemetery, New York.

'Doc' Middleton, rustler, gambler and Wild West performer died in jail in Douglas, Wyoming in 1913. Annie Oakley died in her sleep of pernicious anaemia on 3rd November, 1926 at her home in Greenville. Her husband and manager, Frank Butler, had gone to Detroit and died there twenty days later. His body was brought back to Greenville to be with Annie.

Most of the Indians in the show returned to the reservations and obscurity. Some died during an influenza epidemic while the show was in Spain, as did the orator, Frank Richmond. We have seen how Sitting Bull was killed by Indian police and how Lone Wolf and Paul Eagle Star died while with the Wild West and were buried in England. A few Indians simply faded into the background while with the show in Europe, never to be heard from again. Black Elk returned to the US, and with the help of interpreters, wrote his autobiography including a description of his life with the Wild West and Buffalo Bill.

Cody had many horses during his career and an earlier chapter describes in detail how 'Old Charlie' died and was buried at sea in 1888, when the show left England on the Persian Monarch. A companion to this animal was 'Billy', a big grey that was known as the horse portrayed carrying Buffalo Bill on many of the posters. Returning to America on the steamer, Mohawk, the Wild

West disembarked at Jersey City. Billy was led off the ship by the gangplank, and as soon as his hooves struck American soil, the horse for no apparent reason dropped dead immediately. Like Charlie, Billy had been a favourite of everyone in the show and was mourned as much as any human.

During the Spanish-American War, Cody despatched 'Knickerbocker' and 'Lancer' to Porto Rico in anticipation of his being called into service. When this did not happen the horses were ridden by General Nelson Miles, and after the war were returned to Cody via Washington, the only animals returned to American soil. Knickerbocker was a powerful grey, and Lancer a sorrel, a slightly lighter built horse.

The last horse that Buffalo Bill rode in the Wild West was 'Isham', another grey. When the show was finally auctioned, Isham was put up for sale along with everything else, but friends of Cody elected to purchase the animal and presented it back to him.

The bucking horse 'Dynamite' was injured and had to be destroyed after a train wreck near Lexington in 1900.

So ended the great Wild West. To the fading strains of Mr. Sweeney's cowboy band, Buffalo Bill and his riders drift from history into legend. The fields which once echoed to gunfire and the rumble of the Deadwood Stage now bear the scars of concrete, bricks and mortar. Although some items are still to be found in the hands of private collectors, much that remains of the show now resides in the Buffalo Bill Historical Centre, Wyoming.

Gone are the Cossacks, the Gauchos and the painted warriors of the plains.

We will never see their like again.

**BUFFALO BILL'S WILD WEST
AND
CONGRESS OF ROUGH RIDERS OF THE WORLD**

*J.P. Noble in the uniform of the Texas National Guard 1916/17.*

# RESEARCHING THE WILD WEST

I hope that the reader finds this book as interesting as I did in researching it. Aspects and information on the lives and times of this great show which were once available for a few pennies are sadly now harder to trace. Research of this kind is not for the faint hearted, and those involved know well the disappointments of not being able to find that vital piece of material that only the heart knows survives, somehow, somewhere, in some long forgotten attic.

It may seem surprising, but hardly any photographic evidence has come to light to illustrate the visits of the Wild West to Yorkshire and Lincolnshire. This is specially so, when one bears in mind the fact that Barnum & Bailey's, 'Greatest Show on Earth' toured in a similar fashion around the turn of the century, before the last visit of Buffalo Bill, and photographs of the circus still exist. This negates the suggestion that cameras of the period were unable to capture good images due to motion blur. Many photographs do exist of the show in other parts of the country and many more in the United States. If anyone reading this can shed some light on the whereabouts of images of any aspect of the Wild West in Yorkshire and Lincolnshire, please contact the author via the publishers. This also goes for any printed material concerning the Wild West, and maybe one day I can update this book to its full potential.

I became interested in Buffalo Bill's Wild West entirely by accident when I volunteered to assist my brother with some background information on the family history, a task which he is still wrestling with. All families have interesting stories, which are passed down through the generations, and one in ours, which always held my imagination, was that told me by our paternal grandfather. His early life is still something of a mystery, but slowly unfolding, with connections in Halifax (England), new York, Texas and New Zealand. Even though very young at the time, I can recall the visits to my grandparent's house. It was dark, with dimly lit passageways and eerie alcoves, fearful to a youngster but full of potential adventure and fascinating objects, which were a part of my grandfather's life. We know only a

fraction of his early life, much of it very mysterious and sadly now beyond our reach. I recall the many paintings produced by his skilled hands, both in oils and watercolours, from the Maoris of New Zealand and bare knuckle boxers to the cattle drives of the American Mid West. Unfortunately, most of these have now been lost to us, and we have only a few examples of his work. One is probably the most sensitive, showing an elderly couple on a park bench in Hull's East Park, and is in the possession of my brother.

Although I was only eight years old when he died, looking back, I have the impression that my grandfather, although being very gregarious, often needed his 'own space'. Even during family gatherings at Christmas, he would drift off into the back parlour for a smoke by the fire, often lost within his own thoughts. I still feel much empathy with my grandfather, and sometimes have the same needs. It was at times like this when I would invade his solitude, and I do not recall a single instance when he was too tired or pre-occupied to pull me up onto his knee and tell me about his 'experiences', as we all knew them as.

My grandfather told me of the time when his father had taken him to see Buffalo Bill's Wild West. Apparently, my great grandfather knew Cody and after the show he guided the father and son around the encampment. As the family emigrated to New York from Halifax (and later to New Zealand), this must have happened in the United States, my grandfather being born there in 1885. To continue with the story, Buffalo Bill picked up my grandfather and sat him on his shoulders as they wandered around the grounds. This would certainly be typical of Cody and everything that I recall my grandfather told me of the incident is consistent with what I now know of the Wild West. There is a possibility that my great grandfather may have been involved with the Wild West in a legal capacity and researches continue.

At first, the reader, as I sometimes did as I grew older, may believe this to be just a story told to a child. My researches into the Wild West now convince me that the event did happen. Also, my grandfather was hailed by all who knew him as a person of great integrity, even by political opponents, becoming a

Councillor for the City of Hull and a Chairman of the Hull Trades Council, leading many Mayday Parades. Other aspects of my grandfather's early life are just as interesting and often exciting. I recall him telling me of Butch Cassidy and the Wild Bunch, twenty-five years before Hollywood cashed in on the story. I cannot now recall much about the incidents he told me of or how he came to know of them, but I remember the names, and of Nathan Champion and the Red Sash gang, less well known personalities to all but American historical aficionados.

After a family quarrel, my grandfather left New Zealand and returned to the US, finding himself in the 36th Lone Star Regiment, Texas National Guard. He was trained at Camp Bowie, near Fort Worth and the photograph shows him in pre 1917 uniform. This connects with another memory clip that I have of my grandfather telling me of Pancho Villa and the Mexican Revolution, although the context I have lost. This puts him on the Mexican border around the time that Villa invaded the US and was chased back across the Rio Grande by General Pershing. Some pieces of information suggest that my grandfather may have been a bayonet instructor with the 36th, reinforced by the fact that I recall he had a collection of bayonets in Hull.

There are other pieces of information as yet incomplete that suggest he may have served in other capacities during World War One but are inappropriate here.

And so, for now, the story comes full circle. How many times have I regretted being too young to be aware of the importance of the times spent with my grandfather. How good it would be to regress with perfect recall, and remember the things he told me of far off forests and mountains, scouts and Indians, and Buffalo Bill's Wild West.

James Noble

## Appendix One

Reference - Huddersfield Examiner
Route Book (1896)

|  | Canvas (yrds) | Stakes | Planks |
|---|---|---|---|
| Grandstand | 7,000 | 344 | |
| Toe Pins | | 225 | 2000 |
| Side wall | 5,000 | | |
| Horse Tents | 4,000 | | |
| Dressing Room | 1,500 | 68 | |
| Bronco Tents | | 96 | |
| Baggage Stock | | 68 | |
| Side Show | 2,000 | 38 | |
| Back Wall | | 65 | |
| Dining Tent | 2,500 | 68 | |
| Marquee | 500 | 25 | |
| Banners | | 10 | |
| Electric Light | | 65 | |

Rope - 20 miles

Total show canvas - 23,000 square yards

Total showground workers - 175

Total individual items for construction of showground - 10,000+

Total poles for showground - 4,000

Total stakes for showground - 1,200

## Appendix Two

Illustrations

With grateful thanks to the following : -

Manchester Department of Libraries & Theatres

Mr. David Robinson, York

Mr. & Mrs. D. A. Barber (Programme)

Tyne & Wear Archive Service

Mrs. Elizabeth Knight

Mrs. E. Whitworth

Mr. Robert Shaw of Doncaster

Mr. & Mrs. Paddison of Hull

Also the author's collection

## Appendix Three

From the 10th edition route Book;-

Staff of Buffalo Bill's Wild West

| | |
|---|---|
| Col. W. F. Cody | (President and Director General) |
| John M. Burke | General Manager |
| Johnny Baker | Arenic Director |
| J. Esquivell | Chief of Cowboys |
| F. Dangerfield | Scenic Artist |
| Jule Keen | Business Manager & Treasurer |
| Wm. McCune | Officer of the Day |
| Wm. Sweeney | Leader of the Cowboy Band |
| M.B. Bailey | Chief Electrician |
| L.E. Decker | Representing Col. W. F. Cody |

Press Bureau:

Major John M. Burke
Harvey L. Watkins
Charles S. Wells
Dexter W. Fellows

Staff of Barnum & Bailey Ltd.

| | |
|---|---|
| George O. Starr | Director |
| Fred B. Hutchinson | Manager |
| Alfred D. Starr | Treasurer |
| Clarence L. Dean | General Agent |
| Harvey L. Watkins | General Press Agent |

## Appendix Four

The programme as it appeared in the 10th Edition route Book, 1903

1) OVERTURE - "Star Spangled banner". Cowboy Band. Wm. Sweeney, Director.
2) GRAND REVUE, introducing the Rough Riders of the World. Led by Col. W. F. Cody, "Buffalo Bill".
3) EXHIBITION OF SEATS IN THE SADDLE, by a Cowboy, a Cossack, a Mexican, an Arab, a Gaucho and an Indian
4) ARTILLERY DRILL - Battery D, 5th US Artillery
5) PRAIRIE IMMIGRANT TRAIN CROSSING THE PLAINS the Campfire, the Quadrill on horseback, Attack by Indians and repulsed by Cowboys
6) PONY EXPRESS
7) A GROUP OF MEXICANS - Use of the Lasso
8) JOHNNY BAKER - Marksman
9) COSSACKS - Feats of Horsemanship
10) WESTERN PRAIRIE GIRLS - Riding Display
11) ARAB HORSEMEN - Native Sports and Pastimes
12) COWBOY FUN - Horsemanship and Bronc-riding
13) INDIANS FROM THE SIOUX, ARAPAHOE, BRULE AND CHEYENNE TRIBES - War Dances and a tribal Skirmish
14) MILITARY EXERCISES BY VETERAN ENGLISH CAVALRYMEN
15) VETERANS of the 6th US Cavalry
16) ATTACK ON THE DEADWOOD STAGECOACH
17) RACING BY INDIAN BOYS ON BAREBACK HORSES
18) COL. W.F. CODY, "BUFFALO BILL" - Shooting from the Saddle
19) INFANTRY - THE AURORA (ILLINOIS) ZOUAVES Military Drill
20) RANCH LIFE IN THE WEST - Settler's cabin attacked by Indians and rescue by Buffalo Bill and Cowboys
21) A SALUTE BY THE ENTIRE CONGRESS OF ROUGH RIDERS

FINALE

## Appendix Five

The Wild West Showground

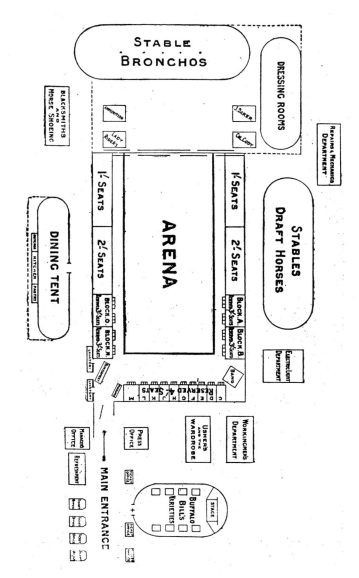